Chapter 2
Designing the Physical Classroom Space for Discussions   23

Whole Class Mathematics Discussions

Improving In-Depth Mathematical Thinking and Learning

Teruni D. Lamberg

University of Nevada, Reno

PEARSON

Boston   Columbus   Indianapolis   New York   San Francisco   Upper Saddle River
Amsterdam   Cape Town   Dubai   London   Madrid   Milan   Munich   Paris   Montréal   Toronto
Delhi   Mexico City   São Paulo   Sydney   Hong Kong   Seoul   Singapore   Taipei   Tokyo

For my wonderful husband, Scott,
our beloved son, Zachary (Zack), & my parents

Senior Editor: Kelly Villella Canton
Editorial Assistant: Annalea Manalili
Executive Marketing Manager: Krista Clark
Production Editor: Karen Mason
Production Coordination and Electronic Composition: Element LLC
Text Design and Illustrations: Element LLC
Cover Coordinator: Jenny Hart
Cover Photo: Theresa Danna-Douglas
Interior Photos: Author photo: Scott Lamberg; interior photos: Theresa Danna-Douglas, Holly Marich, Claudia Bertolone-Smith, and Teruni Lamberg

Library of Congress Cataloging-in-Publication Data
[CIP data not available at time of publication.]

10 9 8 7 6 5 4 3 2 1

ISBN 10: 0-13-211733-9
ISBN 13: 978-0-13-211733-3

Video Clips

Preface

How can you effectively use whole class discussions to support student math learning? How do whole class discussions contribute to student learning? Even though the National Council of Teachers of Mathematics Standards and the Common Core standards point out that communication is crucial part of learning mathematics, many teachers struggle to figure out the best way to help students learn how to communicate math concepts. Implementing these communication standards can be quite challenging because it involves coordinating various ideas from different areas of research, such as understanding how students learn math, teaching for conceptual understanding, lesson planning, using effective questioning strategies, and focusing on student reasoning. This book outlines appropriate strategies for effective whole class discussions that support in-depth mathematical thinking and learning, covers the *thinking process* you need to develop in order to cultivate a community environment in your classroom, and how to design effective standards-based lessons. In addition, this book provides you with the tools and resources to fine tune your discussions and get results in student learning!

Developing a System to Support Whole Class Discussions

Several years ago, when I was teaching elementary school, my school district decided to adopt a National Science Foundation reformed textbook to teach math. The NSF textbook replaced the traditional math textbooks that focused on teaching students problem solving procedures. The new textbook went far beyond simple calculations and step-by-step procedures. We were expected to engage students in mathematical thinking and help them understand concepts behind equations. Moving from procedures to conceptual learning meant a fundamental shift in the way we taught, and it was quite a challenge for me and my grade-level teammates.

To overcome our struggles, we started to work with a math coach. Early on, my math coach observed me teaching a lesson on comparing fractions. The previous day, I had covered how to represent a fraction using standard notation. All my students had to do in this lesson was to compare fractions and place them on a number line from least to the greatest, theoretically building on the previous day's lesson. To my dismay, students did not seem to remember my lesson on standard notation! I tried to explain the concept again, but it threw off the course of my lesson. Afterward, I debriefed with my math coach. She asked me to evaluate the student work and to explain how the students were thinking. I proceeded to tell her how many students got the correct answer, and how many students did not. She re-phrased the question and asked me to look at the student work and explain to her what my students understood about a fraction. I noticed that the students had not drawn the same size units and that some students did not understand how to write the fraction or the meaning of a fraction.

As I worked with my math coach, and took graduate college classes to improve my math teaching skills, I began to understand the power of whole class discussions and communication in math. As I found research regarding classroom techniques that support student learning through whole class discussions, I tried new things and changed the way I was teaching. I began to get results! My students appeared to really grasp the concepts, instead of simply repeating procedures or guessing.

Through my classroom experience, graduate school, and the extensive research that supports communication as a means to support learning, I began to understand that students learn math more effectively through communicating. When they discuss their ideas, listen to different perspectives, and engage in sense-making, they deepen their understanding of mathematics. My original teaching methods involved showing students the "steps" to get the correct answer. However, mathematics actually involved thinking; it was more than following a series of steps and memorizing formulas. Mathematics is a "dynamic discipline focused on solving problems by thinking creatively, finding patterns, and reasoning logically" (Bray, 2011). It was necessary to rethink what it meant to understand and learn mathematics, and to change my teaching approaches to incorporate a problem-solving approach that focused on student understanding. Whole class discussions became necessary to effectively support my students as they learned math.

While this change did not happen overnight, the learning process was amazing; I discovered that as I transformed the way I was thinking and teaching math, my students became more motivated to learn math and they became better math students. Teaching math became easier because I was able to meet students' diverse learning needs through discussion. My goal in *Whole Class Mathematics Discussions: Improving In-Depth Mathematical Thinking and Learning* is to share some of these strategies with you.

Testing Whole Class Discussions

To fully develop my ideas about whole class discussions, I did a study on how children learn fractions and specifically looked at how discussions contributed to student learning. My post-doctoral work at Vanderbilt University with Dr. Paul Cobb involved working with teachers across the county, observing discussions, talking to teachers, and thinking about how to support teachers transitioning to discussion based learning. *Whole Class Mathematics Discussions: Improving In-Depth Mathematical Thinking and Learning* was born from the lack of resources supporting teachers as they move to teaching math through communication. The Vanderbilt Project teachers inspired me to think more deeply about the effectiveness and usefulness of whole class discussions.

After I completed my Postdoctorate at Vanderbilt University, I moved to Nevada and became the Principal Investigator in the Northeastern Nevada Mathematics Project, a Math and Science Partnership award funded by the Nevada Department of Education and the U.S. Department of Education. The goal of the project was to provide professional development that actually impacted student learning. We worked hard to figure out how to help teachers improve whole class discussions. We discovered that, as teachers, we need to have a *reason* to change how we teach; we need to know that it will help increase student learning and improve test scores; we need to understand *how* discussion actually supports learning before we decide to make changes in our teaching; and we need to be *aware* of the impact our actions have on student learning. Being aware of our actions and their impact means developing a lens for examining our teaching. *Whole Class Mathematics Discussions* provides that lens. Inside, you'll not only find information on how to facilitate effective whole class discussions, but also resources and tools to support self-examination of the impact you have on your classroom throughout this journey.

The tools in *Whole Class Mathematics Discussions* are tried and true; as the current principal investigator and director of the Lemelson Math and Science Master's cohort program, I have encouraged several teachers to test many strategies in the book. Lemelson Cohort I & Cohort II teachers have tried out many of the ideas and tools presented in this book and provided continuous constructive feedback. Three of these teachers are featured in the video cases presented in this book, and the teacher planning photos feature some of the Lemelson cohort teachers.

How to Use This Edition

This book is designed to help you facilitate effective whole class discussions that support in-depth mathematical thinking. Effective whole class discussions increase student understanding and learning of mathematics. Although the ideas presented in this book specifically cover math discussions, they can be adapted to other content areas as well. This book is intended to be used and re-used as a tool. You may be an experienced teacher who is interested in fine tuning your discussion. Or perhaps you are a pre-service teacher who is just starting the journey of becoming a teacher. Maybe, you are a math coach, a professional development coordinator, or a professor who is interested in supporting others as they implement effective whole class discussions. Use this book as an individual resource or as part of a study group. Furthermore, you can customize the book by choosing which tools you use and adapting them to meet your specific needs.

Chapter one provides you with an overview of the thinking process needed to facilitate effective whole class discussion. Each subsequent chapter describes various aspects of this process by synthesizing the research and providing practical strategies that can be directly applied in the classroom. Chapter Six addresses how to evaluate your areas of strengths and weaknesses in order to refine and fine-tune your whole class discussions. Each chapter contains the following features:

- A synthesis of research applied to specific topics with concrete examples of how teachers have already applied the concepts in their classrooms.

- **Study Guide:** Provides you with guidelines on how to use the tools and resources in the accompanying PDToolkit to deepen your understanding of the key ideas presented in each chapter, make connections to real classrooms, and offer practical suggestions to try out ideas in real classrooms. The study guide can be used individually or as a group.

- **Video and Classroom Case Studies:** In-depth case studies offer a close look at how real teachers use the strategies from the chapter to teach mathematical concepts. Interviews with both students and teachers provide interesting insights to the outcome of whole class discussions.

- **Strategies for Your Classroom:** This bulleted list offers strategies that you can directly apply in the classroom based on the ideas discussed in the chapter. A full-page PDF of this page is also available for download from PDToolkit.

- **Self-Reflection Questions:** A series of questions designed to help you reflect on your classroom.

PDToolkit for *Whole Class Mathematics Discussions: Improving In-Depth Mathematical Thinking and Learning*

Purchase of *Whole Class Mathematics Discussions* includes access to PDToolkit, a website with media resources that, together with the text, provide the tools you need to fully explore and implement the concepts presented in the book. The PDToolkit for *Whole Class Mathematics Discussions: Improving In-Depth Mathematical Thinking and Learning* is available free for six months after you register using the access code that comes with this book. After that, it is available by subscription for a yearly fee. Be sure to explore and download (as noted) the following resources:

PD **pd** TOOLKIT™
for
Whole Class Mathematics Discussions

- **Video Clips:** The video clips referenced throughout the text can be viewed on PDTookit; they include examples of whole class discussions, teacher interviews, and student interviews from a variety of grade levels and schools.

- **End of Chapter Worksheets, Rubrics, Self-Evaluations Tools, and Questions for Discussion.** (Some of these work sheets are writable PDFs.) The downloadable worksheets and forms fall into the following four broad categories:

  - ❖ **Strategies for Your Classroom.** Key ideas from each chapter are provided in a bulleted list as specific strategies that can be tried out in the classroom. The teacher can post these ideas and use them during lesson planning and reference them during the lesson.

  - ❖ **Reflecting on Video Clips.** Questions are provided to encourage critical thinking about each video. These questions correspond to the content presented in each chapter.

  - ❖ **Reflecting on Practice.** Questions are provided to help the teacher identify strengths and weaknesses in whole class discussions. Once areas for growth are identified, the book and other resources can be used as support to improve teaching.

❖ **Rubrics and Checklists.** These tools are designed to monitor and provide feedback on classroom discussions.

❖ **PowerPoints:** Each PowerPoint synthesizes the key idea from each chapter and contains the corresponding Video Clips for the chapter. It also provides questions for discussion or reflection.

○ The PowerPoint can be used as a study guide for each chapter and functions as an outline of the key ideas presented in each chapter. The reader can print out the PowerPoint and make notes on it while reading the chapter.

○ The PowerPoints can also be used in Classrooms, Book Study Groups, and professional development sessions as talking points to explore the ideas presented in the book.

How to Adapt this Book for Pre-Service Teachers

Whole Class Mathematics Discussions: Improving In-Depth Mathematical Thinking and Learning provides pre-service students with an image of what a whole class discussion that supports learning looks like. It also provides insights into planning lessons with discussions in mind, making this book a great resource when they enter the classroom. As students, the pre-service teachers can read each chapter in sequence to learn about the thinking process needed to facilitate effective discussion. Their instructors can use the videos and study guide questions to reflect on key ideas of chapters and generate discussions on how to facilitate effective whole class discussions. My pre-service teachers found the tools provided in this book to be helpful in both preparing for service and in understanding what a mathematical discussion actually looks like. Whole class discussion strategies are easily embedded and modeled throughout the math methods course. Using this method, pre-service teachers will gain experience with discussions by developing lessons and presenting them in their methods classes. Then, the rest of the class can debrief and reflect on the effectiveness of discussions and mathematical learning they experienced. This book is also an excellent supplement to any field experience class where pre-service students are working with real students.

CourseSmart, eBook, and other eBook Options Available

CourseSmart is an exciting new choice for purchasing *Whole Class Mathematics Discussions: Improving In-Depth Mathematical Thinking and*

Learning. As an alternative to purchasing the printed book, you now have the choice of purchasing an electronic version via CourseSmart that can be read on PCs and MACs, and for on-the-go reading, on Android devices, iPads, iPhones and iPod Touches with CourseSmart Apps. With a CourseSmart eBook, readers can search the text, make notes online, print out reading assignments that incorporate lecture notes, and bookmark important passages for later review. For more information or to purchase access to the CourseSmart eBook, visit http://www.coursesmart.com. Also look for this book on a number of eBook devices and platforms.

Acknowledgments

I would like to thank my editor Kelly Villella Canton for her support and belief in me as I went through the journey of completing this manuscript. She always provided encouragement, helpful suggestions, and constructive feedback. I would also like to thank Karen Mason, the Production Editor, for her continuous constructive feedback and her hard work ensuring a smooth production process. I am very grateful for all the copyediting work done by Janet Stone and B-Books. They were wonderful to work with and certainly brought this manuscript to life! There are many others who were involved in the production of this book: the team at Pearson (including Aurora Martinez, Molly Bagshaw, Krista Clark, Megan Cochran, Caroline Fenton, Jenny Hart, Sacha Laustsen, Annalea Manalili, and Ginny Michaud) and the team at Element LLC (including Susan McNally and Cindy Miller). I appreciate all their hard work and support.

I am grateful to the following mentors and individuals who shaped my thinking about whole class discussions: Dr. James Middleton and Wendy Kubasko, Dr. Paul Cobb, Dr. Kay McClain, Peggy Glick, Dave Brancamp, Sharon Mclean, Gini Cunnigham, Dr. Chaiten Gupta, Peggy Lakey and Lou Loftin.

Ms. Dotty Lemelson funded two math and science cohorts at the University of Nevada, Reno. Cohort I & Cohort II teachers actively tried out many of the ideas and tools presented in this book and provided constructive feedback. Three of these teachers are featured in the video cases presented in this book. In addition, some of these teachers are featured in the photos throughout this book. I am thankful to Ms. Dotty Lemelson for her support in funding such a program to improve math education in Nevada and across the country. In addition, I am grateful for the support of the Lemelson cohort teachers and Caryn Swobe, President at Swobe Strategies.

Not only did I receive feedback from practicing teachers, I also gained valuable insight from pre-service teachers in my math methods and practicum courses. I learned from my pre-service students that having an image of what a discussion looks like is valuable for them. Their feedback inspired me to capture real classrooms in the format of video clips.

I am thankful to Claudia Bertolone-Smith, Marlene Moyer, Kelsey Rivara, Megan Tilton, Channon Toles, and Bonnie Akbar, who were gracious enough to let me record them. Their classrooms are featured in the video cases in this book as examples of whole class discussions. They truly are dedicated teachers who care about teaching and about helping other teachers. These are real classrooms. You can learn so many things by watching real classrooms, particularly what worked well in class and what challenges the teachers faced. I am also grateful for the support of Wendy Kubasko from Pedergast School District. Her passion for teaching and making a difference is inspirational.

The manuscript developed out of many ideas. I appreciate the many conversations with and constructive feedback I received from teachers and others during the process of writing my manuscript. A special thank you to Annalissa Walker, Diana Moss, Denise Trakas, Claudia Bertolone-Smith, Bonnie Akbar, Julie Amador, Holly Marich, and Lynda Wiest. In addition, I would like to thank Our Lady of the Snows Parochial School in Reno, NV, Washoe School District, Douglas School District, White Pine School District, Humboldt School District, Elko County School District, Eureka School District, and Lander County School Districts in Nevada. Also, I am grateful to the support of Madison School district in Arizona and Durham Public Schools in North Carolina.

A special thank you for the reviewers, lined up by Pearson, who have taken the time to read and comment on the proposal, chapters, and drafts of this manuscript. Your insights and contributions have shaped the final product. We thank all of the following reviewers: Kristi Anderson, Lake Hamilton School District; Susan Avant, Liberty County Schools; Danielle Bouton-Wales, Schenectady City School District; Julie Carter, Emerson Taylor School District; Denise Justice, Raceland Worthington Independent School District; Jennifer Law, Klein Independent School District; Mona Toncheff, Phoenix Union High School District; Cathy Williams, San Diego County Office of Education; and Sarah Woofter, Collier County Public Schools.

I would also like to thank my parents who inspired me by saying that anything was possible to achieve if you set your mind to it. Finally, I could not have done this without the love and support of my husband and son! They mean the world to me.

Why Whole Class Discussions?

As students are asked to communicate about the mathematics they are studying—to justify their reasoning to classmates or formulate a question about something that is puzzling—they gain insights into their thinking. In order to communicate their thinking to others, students naturally reflect on their learning and organize and consolidate their thinking about the mathematics.

(NCTM, Principals and Standards)

Teachers interested in helping students learn math more effectively have many questions when approached with the concept of using whole class discussions to facilitate understanding mathematics: What do students gain from whole class discussions? How can you support students in learning math through whole class discussions? What do you need to do in order to effectively use whole class discussions in your classroom? By asking these questions, teachers are able to explore what research already shows: that students learn math through communicating. When they discuss their ideas, listen to different perspectives, and engage in sense-making, students deepen their understanding of mathematics. Mathematics is more than following a series of steps and memorizing formulas. Mathematics is a "dynamic discipline focused on solving problems by thinking creatively, finding patterns, and reasoning

logically" (Bray, 2011). Teaching through a problem-solving approach that focuses on student understanding can help students learn math.

Whole class discussions to support student learning are essential in NCTM standards-based programs (Kazemi & Stipek, 2001; Stein, Engle, Smith, Hughes, 2008). My goal in this book is to share effective whole class discussion strategies that will help you support your students as they learn mathematics with conceptual understanding. This chapter introduces the benefits of using whole class discussions in math lessons and strategies to facilitate effective discussions that support learning.

Common Core and NCTM Standards

The Common Core State standards for Mathematics and the National Council of Teachers of Mathematics (NCTM) standards highlight the importance of communication in helping students develop deep understanding of mathematical ideas and their ability to proficiently solve problems. To meet these standards, students must be actively engaged in the process of learning mathematics. The standards cover not only the mathematical concepts that students should learn, but also outline an approach for teaching mathematics. For example, the Common Core standards include eight mathematical practices detailing how students should learn mathematics. These eight practices also align with the NCTM process standards. In both the Common Core State and NCTM standards, communication is an essential part of how students should learn math, as shown in this Common Core standard of mathematical practices:

> **3. Construct viable arguments and critique the reasoning of others.**
>
> Mathematically proficient students understand and use stated assumptions, definitions, and previously established results in constructing arguments. They make conjectures and build a logical progression of statements to explore the truth of their conjectures. They are able to analyze situations by breaking them into cases and can recognize counter-examples. They justify their conclusions and communicate them to others and respond to the argument of others. . . . (CCSSO & NGA, 2010)

According to the Common Core State standards, students must be able to explain and justify their thinking. In addition, students should be able to explain why a mathematical statement is true or how a mathematical rule works.

NCTM process standards integrate problem solving, reasoning and proof, communication, and representations. The NCTM (2000) Communication standard states that students should be able to:

- organize and consolidate their mathematical thinking through communication
- communicate their mathematical thinking coherently and clearly to peers, teachers and others
- analyze and evaluate the mathematical thinking and strategies of others
- use the language of mathematics to express ideas precisely

By focusing on how students can communicate mathematical concepts, both the Common Core State standards and the NCTM standards naturally support a whole class discussion approach to teaching math. It will allow students to develop more efficient mathematical thinking and to build on concepts they have discovered through effective, guided communication.

Whole Class Discussion and Student Achievement

Whole class discussions take time. Many teachers wonder if the time spent on whole class discussion is justified, especially when so much content must be covered in a short period of time. However, when students develop conceptual understanding of mathematical ideas, they retain what they learn and develop greater skills in math. If students forget how to solve a problem, they can figure it out if they understand the concepts behind the problem. On the other hand, when students simply memorize problem-solving procedures without understanding how or why they work, they are more likely to have difficulty remembering how to do problems (Kilpatrick, Swafford & Bradford, 2001). For example, students who memorize that $9 + 9 = 18$ without understanding what it means are less likely to apply that type of problem solving to additional problems. Helping students understand mathematical concepts (known as having number sense) allows students to make mathematical connections and successfully solve problems using efficient strategies.

Whole class discussions can help students develop their number sense. Researchers have found that focusing on different reasoning strategies leads to higher mathematical insights (Stein, Engle, Smith & Hughes, 2008; Leinhardt & Steele, 2005). Furthermore, students who learn math through an effective standards-based approach (such as the Common Core or NCTM standards) do well in math achievement tests and outperform students who are taught using traditional approaches in problem-solving tasks (Schoenfeld, 2002).

Schoenfeld (2002) points out that these approaches to teaching also narrow the achievement gap among English language learners. When these students have the opportunity to speak in their first language for a few minutes, transition to English, and connect the words to visual representations, they make vocabulary connections (Wiest, 2008). ELLs are faced with learning a second language at the same time that they are learning the content. Therefore, teachers need to think about students' language goals as well as the mathematical goals (Bresser, Melanese & Sphar, 2009). Teachers can do this by identifying vocabulary that they are unfamiliar with and find ways to build discussion based on what students know. This strategy is useful for helping all students communicate around difficult math vocabulary until they have firmly grasped the new concept. Once they conceptually understand the lesson, integrating the math vocabulary will give students greater math communication abilities and help them meet state standards.

Communication and Mathematical Learning

The National Research Council has identified five strands for mathematical proficiency (Kilpatrick, Swafford, & Findell, 2001):*

1. *conceptual understanding*—comprehension of mathematical concepts, operations, and relations
2. *procedural fluency*—skill in carrying out procedures flexibly, accurately, efficiently, and appropriately
3. *strategic competence*—ability to formulate, represent, and solve mathematical problems
4. *adaptive reasoning*—capacity for logical thought, reflection, explanation, and justification
5. *productive disposition*—habitual inclination to see mathematics as sensible, useful, and worthwhile, coupled with a belief in diligence and one's own efficacy.

All five strands require communication. Consider the requirements for reflection and explanation in the fourth strand, adaptive reasoning. When students share their reasoning and listen to different perspectives, they engage in *reflective* thought. Reflective thought involves carefully analyzing what is being said, making judgments, and understanding how

*Kilpatrick, Swafford & Findell (Eds.). (2001). *Adding It Up: Helping Children Learn Mathematics.* p. 116. Reprinted with Permission.

that new information fits with prior knowledge. On the other hand, if new information does not fit, reflective thought requires that existing ideas be adjusted with the new ones (Fosnot, 2005). Typically, new learning and deeper understanding result from this reflective thinking process. By sharing, explaining, and justifying ideas, students develop skills in reasoning and engage in sense-making.

"Math Talk" with Partners, Small Groups, and Whole Class

There are many different types of communication that can take place during a math lesson, such as talk with partners, small groups, and the whole class. Each type of "math talk" serves a different purpose and contributes to the development of new mathematical insights. For example, students can brainstorm or clarify ideas with partners, small groups, or the teacher, and discuss ideas as a group to explore a topic in more depth. Although this book focuses on whole class discussions, it also explains the importance of working with partners or small groups to allow students to individually share their thinking, get specific feedback on their ideas, and reflect on other ideas. The drawback of partner or small group talk is that students are limited to the perspective of the partner or small group. Students may not be able to solve problems themselves and clear up any misconceptions during these conversations without the additional support of a whole class discussion.

Case Study: Problem Solving with Partners

A first-grade class is asked to share their strategies with a partner for adding 9 + 9. Melissa uses counters to solve the problem. She takes 9 blocks out of a basket and places them on her desk. Then she takes out another 9 blocks, places them on the table, and starts counting by pointing to the blocks. However, since she is not physically moving the blocks, she loses track of which blocks she has counted and gets the answer 15.

   Her partner, Martin, also takes out 9 blocks. Then he takes another 9 blocks and adds them to the first 9 blocks to make one large pile. He carefully moves each block to the other side of the table and counts them one at a time. After counting all the blocks, he concludes that the answer is 18. Noticing that both students have

Continues on next page

Case Study, continued

different answers, the teacher asks Melissa and Martin to figure out which answer is correct. They start by placing all the blocks in the basket and then counting out two piles of 9 blocks. Martin gathers the blocks together and moves the pieces while Melissa counts. They both conclude that the answer should be 18. Even though Melissa changes her mind that the answer should be 18, she does not realize that she needs to explicitly think about more efficient ways to keep track while she counts.

At another table, Zack and Reilly use completely different strategies. Zack takes out only 9 blocks. He explains to Reilly, "I started with the number 9 and counted up to get the answer (18)." Reilly tells Zack that she figured out her answer in a different way. She tells Zack that $9 + 1$ make 10. Therefore, she re-conceptualizes the problem as $10 + 8 = 18$.

ANALYSIS: The partner discussion allowed students to discuss and articulate their thinking to their partners, but it would have been beneficial to hear how other students solved the problem. Martin and Melissa could have demonstrated how they counted 18 blocks; Zack could have shown why he counted 9 blocks, which was more efficient than Martin's way. Reilly could explain how her approach was similar to Zack's, because she re-conceptualized the problem. The rest of the students could listen, ask questions, explain thinking, and make their own connections to deepen their understanding of addition strategies and develop their number sense.

The richness of a whole class discussion is dependent on the quality of small group and partner conversations that take place first. The small group discussion and partner talks generate a rich background of ideas for a whole class discussion. These smaller discussions activate prior knowledge and engage students in thinking about the lesson. Then, during the whole class discussion, students are exposed to multiple perspectives that stretch their thinking. The teacher's role is to pose questions and scaffold the discussion by making decisions about how to sequence or facilitate the discussion so that there is a logical progression of ideas that everyone can understand. Eventually, the teacher wants all her students, through reflecting on the various ideas presented, to develop more efficient strategies and deeper understanding of math concepts.

SELF-REFLECTION QUESTIONS

1. What kinds of math talk currently takes place in your classroom?

2. When do you use partner talk, small group talk, and whole class discussions?

3. What is your purpose in using these different kinds of talk?

A Peek Inside the Classroom

Video Clip 1.1 Student Interview: Student Perspectives on "Math Talk" and Math Learning (00:01:55)

In Video Clip 1.1, Student Interview: Student Perspectives on "Math Talk" and Math Learning, students in a fifth-grade and sixth-grade class explain how "math talk" contributes to mathematical learning. When they discuss their ideas with a partner, it helps them reflect on their own thinking and self-correct any mistakes. Furthermore, it helps them get started on problem solving by clarifying any information they don't understand. Listening to multiple perspectives during the whole group discussion stretches their thinking. One student said that when she was working with her partner, they were following the wrong path to solve the problem. However, when they listened to the whole group, they were able to understand what they were doing wrong and self-correct.

PD ❿ TOOLKIT™

for *Whole Class Mathematics Discussions*

View the video online at PDToolkit.

Their perspective is consistent with existing research. Talk helps students to understand mathematics more deeply and with greater clarity (Chapin, O'Conner & Anderson, 2009).

Video Clip 1.2, Fifth & Sixth Grade Teacher Perspectives on Class Discussions, contains an interview with two teachers who team-teach the students in Video Clip 1.1. Ms. Bertolone-Smith and Ms. Malone combine their fifth- and sixth-grade classes to teach math. Ms. Bertolone-Smith believes that whole class discussion is the most important part of the math lesson because students listen to multiple perspectives, clarify their thinking, and even change their answers. Ms. Bertolone-Smith and Ms. Malone also find that students are motivated to learn when they are mentally engaged. When students have

Video Clip 1.2 Fifth & Sixth Grade Teacher Perspectives on Class Discussions (0:04:05)

PD TOOLKIT™

for *Whole Class Mathematics Discussions*

View the video online at PDToolkit.

had time to think about a problem individually and in small groups, they are ready and eager to share their thinking during the discussion.

> *Ms. Bertolone-Smith:* They learn so much from watching their peers discuss and analyze the problem. If Marlene or I were to get up there and say, "this is how it is," you would see them all fade into the background. But when they are listening to their peers describe mathematics that they have engaged in, they are just interested. . . . They are wondering, "What does another person see in the problem that I didn't?" That is a really rich discussion versus, "I am going to come up and show you the right answer."

> *Ms. Malone:* That piece of "can I listen to their reasoning, can I let go of my reasoning because my reasoning isn't clear, am I willing to hear someone else and say, Oh I see it!," This is where some of the most profound changes happen. . . . You notice that we never say what the answer is until it is basically so obvious. . . . Eventually at the end we allow kids to change their answers and I think that is very powerful.

Students need to listen with an open mind and be willing to change their answer if it does not make sense. The whole class discussion opens students to different possibilities that they may not have thought about individually or with small groups. The social interaction leads students to think, reflect, and refine their thought processes (Chapin, O'Conner & Anderson, 2009).

The teachers state that they create "depth and richness in discussion" when they begin with small group and partner talk, and then build a whole class discussion. Partner talk and small group discussion involves fertilizing a topic. When students think about a problem individually and talk with partners and small groups they are throwing themselves at the problem, and making their ideas explicit without needing to be right. This step is critical in building productive whole class discussions. Teachers have found that when students are not given time to think about a problem, the whole class discussion does not work well. Students may not participate in the discussion or give meaningful responses and the teacher is left struggling to explain the ideas.

Characteristics of Effective Whole Class Discussions

Students develop an understanding of math when they talk about math, listen to others, and observe a variety of representations (Wiest, 2008). Whole class discussions must lead to the development of a more sophisticated understanding of mathematics and build on student thinking by addressing different strategies and errors that students make. Classroom discussion time must be used effectively and efficiently. Table 1.1 distinguishes characteristics of two discussions, one that supports conceptual understanding and one that does not.

The biggest difference between these types of discussions is the purpose of discussion. The main purpose of a whole class discussion is to help students develop a conceptual understanding of mathematics and more efficient strategies through mathematical reasoning and sense-making. Students in a whole class discussion that supports mathematical learning are active participants. The discussion builds on student responses (Stein et al. 2008). Let's look at a few characteristics of effective class discussions that support learning.

Students Develop "Shared" Understanding of a Problem. Students in the whole class discussion develop a shared understanding of a problem or

TABLE **1.1**

Characteristics of Effective and Ineffective Whole Class Discussions

Effective Discussion	Ineffective Discussion
Discussion is open ended with many opportunities for students to present multiple perspectives.	Discussion is closed, with only one right approach for solving the problem.
Students engage in sense-making and explore a problem or issue.	Students passively listen to the teacher.
The purpose of the discussion is to explore and understand a mathematical problem or issue.	Teacher shows students the steps on how to solve problems. Students copy and use the steps to solve problems without understanding why.
Teacher acts as a facilitator by scaffolding the discussion in order to lead students to make connections. Students explore how to solve problems and understand why the approach works.	Teacher explains steps to problem solving as students listen passively or give the correct answers without further discussion.

issue when they offer their perspectives and ask for clarification if they don't understand something that is being discussed (Cobb, Wood & Yackel, 1993; Franke, Webb & Chan, 2009). This shared understanding allows students to explore a problem and progressively deepen their understanding through discussion. They develop new mathematical insights by discussing errors and misconceptions, and exploring why an idea does or does not make sense (Bray, 2011; Kazemi & Stipek, 2001). Whole class discussions are also appropriate when the teacher is introducing a new concept or is challenging students to think deeper about something they already know.

Teachers Provide Students with "Guided Intervention." Whole class discussions provide teachers with the opportunity for "guided intervention" (Gravemeijer & van Galen, 2003). Students don't necessarily discover efficient strategies or deeper mathematical understandings on their own. Therefore, class time can be efficiently used when the teacher uses questions to guide students to think about structured concepts and problems in addition to the questions students raise themselves.

Students Evaluate and Analyze Their Thinking and Their Peers' Thinking. The NCTM standards (2000) state that discussion should involve analyzing and evaluating mathematical thinking of others. Students must think about how to approach the problem as well as understand how other students approach it. Whole class discussions must engage students in critical thinking (Chapin, O'Conner & Anderson, 2009; Smith & Stein, 2011). If students think that the teacher is the only one with the correct answer, they are not likely to be mentally engaged.

Planning a Whole Class Discussion

Orchestrating an effective whole class discussion involves planning the lesson, identifying a topic and a problem for discussion, allowing students to share reasoning, and using guided questions to facilitate the discussion. The whole class discussion must be situated in larger mathematical goals. The discussion has three phases: (1) making thinking explicit, (2) analyzing each other's solutions, and (3) developing new mathematical insights. Table 1.2 briefly describes the process of planning and facilitating an effective whole class discussion. The following chapters discuss each phase in more detail and are supported by Video Clips that demonstrate the process in action. Teacher and student interviews illustrate the process of planning a lesson and impact on student learning.

TABLE **1.2**

The Process of Planning and Conducting an Effective Whole Class Discussion

Planning Prior to Discussion	Identify long-term and short-term goals, consider curricular tasks, and anticipate student reasoning.
Planning During the Lesson	Assess student reasoning/errors/misconceptions. Identify topic for discussion/problem to discuss and think about how to sequence discussion.
Whole Class Discussion: Facilitating Mathematical Connections	Pose question/issue to start discussion. Phase 1: Making thinking explicit Phase 2: Analyzing solutions Phase 3: Developing new mathematical insights. The teacher facilitates the discussion through questioning.

Planning Prior to Discussion

A whole class discussion focuses on one concept or goal; however, it is also part of a larger conversation that takes place over time. When students see connections within a lesson and across lessons, they develop deeper mathematical connections. Therefore, planning begins with setting a clear goal and purpose that fits in with the larger purpose. (Chapter 4 discusses lesson planning and sequencing in more detail.) During the planning process the teacher identifies the concepts and skills that students should develop and selects tasks for students to engage in. In addition, the teacher anticipates student reasoning, errors, and misconceptions that can emerge during the lesson.

PD TOOLKIT™

for *Whole Class Mathematics Discussions*

View the video online at PDToolkit.

A Peek Inside the Classroom

Video Clip 1.3, Fifth & Sixth Grade Teacher Interview on Lesson Planning, shows the thinking process that Ms. Bertolone-Smith and Ms. Malone engaged in as they planned the lesson. They chose a rich multi-step problem (see the study guide at the end of this chapter) that required students to make drawings to visualize the problem and represent their thinking. They anticipated the possible errors and misconceptions that students might make.

Video Clip 1.3 Fifth & Sixth Grade Teacher Interview on Lesson Planning (00:01:20)

Their long-term mathematical goal involved teaching students to engage in problem solving and mathematical reasoning and to use schematic drawings as a part of their problem-solving process.

Planning the Discussion During the Lesson

A problem-solving approach to teaching is necessary for discussion. In Video Clip 1.3, the teacher starts the lesson by posing a problem, giving students time to think about the problem, then meeting with partners or small groups to further explore the problem. During this small group time, the teacher monitors student understanding by asking probing questions and evaluating work. In this phase of the lesson, the teacher makes a quick decision about what to talk about during the whole class discussion based on student reasoning.

Ms. Bertolone-Smith starts the lesson by introducing a multi-step problem on the interactive white board and having students read it aloud: *A picture 3 feet across hangs in the center of a wall that is 25 feet long. How many feet from the left end of the wall is the left edge of the picture?*

> Ms. B: I want you to picture a wall with a painting in the center. Now we are going to use a schematic drawing to find [the answer to the problem].

PD ꝏ TOOLKIT™
for *Whole Class
Mathematics
Discussions*
View the video online
at PDToolkit.

As students work with partners and small groups and use their math journals to record their thinking, the teachers walk around, observing what the students are doing and posing questions.

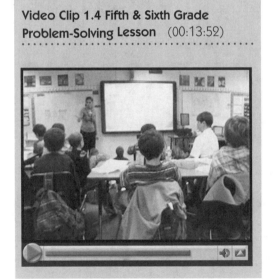

Video Clip 1.4 Fifth & Sixth Grade Problem-Solving Lesson (00:13:52)

The Whole Class Discussion: Facilitating Mathematical Connections

After students have individually thought about a problem and shared ideas with partners or a small group, a whole class discussion takes place.

A Peek Inside the Classroom

Video Clip 1.4, Fifth & Sixth Grade Problem-Solving Lesson, shows the whole class discussion that took place in Ms. Bertolone-Smith and Ms. Malone's classroom.

Students face the interactive white board as Ms B calls for answers and records responses: 11, 10, 12,

11½ and 10½ ft. In a class of 57 students, the range of five different answers represents five different ways of thinking about the problem. These answers become the focus of discussion as opposed to one student's thinking. Now, the solutions that yielded the answers become a class issue for discussion. Ms. Bertolone-Smith asks for a volunteer to defend his answer.

Phase 1: Making Thinking Explicit.
Students explain how they arrived at their answers. Brandon explains his thinking as he displays his drawing, shown here as Figure 1.1, and draws on the interactive white board.

Brandon draws one wall and visualizes the rectangle in the middle as representing the 3-foot painting. He subtracts 3 feet from 25 feet to figure out how much wall space is available that is not covered by the painting. He then divides the free wall space by two and concludes that the answer should be 11.

He accidentally writes the division number sentence backward. When the teacher asks him to check his work, he is able to self-correct.

Phase 2: Analyzing Each Other's Solutions.
Brinn shares her solution and explains how it is similar to and different from Brandon's solution. She came up with the same answer as Brandon but visualized the problem differently.

Brinn's visualization of the problem is different than Brandon's, as you can see in Figure 1.2. She viewed the painting as being placed in the center of a 25-foot wall. She figured out the center of the wall and subtracted half the painting width to find the answer.

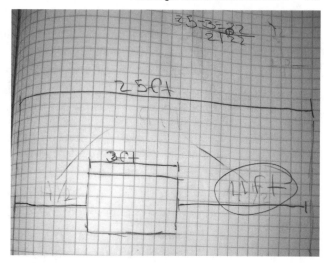

FIGURE **1.1**

Brandon's schematic drawing

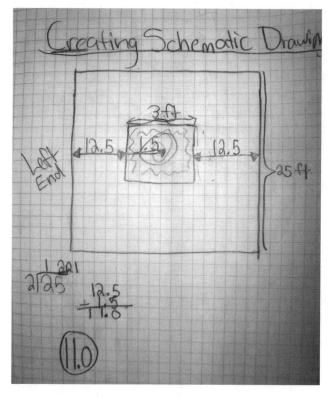

FIGURE **1.2**

Brinn's schematic drawing

After Brinn explains her thinking, the teacher asks students to think about their answers and asks students if anyone wants to change their original answers. By doing so, the teacher communicates to the group that not only should they be listening to other students' answers, but they should also be reflecting if their answer makes sense. Students are expected to reflect on what they see and hear with their own thinking processes.

Nancy: I would like to change my answer from 11.5 to 11. (Another student also decides to change her answer from 12.5 to 11.)

Teacher: Can you tell me why you changed your answer? Tell us why you changed your answer from 12½ to 11.

Student: If the picture frame takes up 3 feet of the wall, then you subtract 3 feet from 25.

Teacher: What did you do before that caused you to arrive at your original answer?

Student: I did not subtract the picture frame from the wall.

Teacher: You did not subtract the 1½ from the 12.5, which got you to the 11. Is that right?

Student: Yeah.

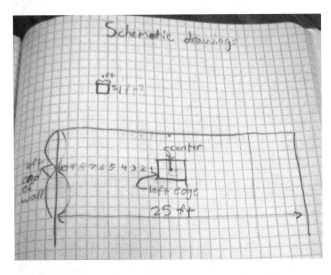

FIGURE 1.3

Ethan's Schematic Drawing

In this example, the students share their thinking and reflect on their own answers. The student could explain how he got a different answer of 12.5. In addition, he could provide a reason for changing his answer based on listening to other students' explanations. The teacher restated what the student said and asked for clarification. The teachers encouraged students to change their answers based on the new insights they gained.

Misconceptions and errors can be addressed through discussion. The whole class discussion gives students opportunities to discuss why something does or does not make sense. For example, the teacher calls on Ethan to present his alternate way to think about the problem and why he thinks the answer is 10 feet. Ethan comes up to the interactive board to present his solution (see Figure 1.3). He uses the grid squares to represent one foot in his schematic drawing and counts out 25 squares. Next, he finds the center of the wall is 12.5 squares from the left edge, and he splits the center square in half. He then proceeds to figure out where the edge of the picture frame is by counting 1.5 squares from the center point of his diagram. His answer represents the number of feet from the edge of the picture frame to the end of the left wall.

> *Teacher:* Does anyone have any questions for Ethan about his drawing? Ethan, take a couple of questions from people who maybe don't understand your thinking clearly. (Several students raise hands.) Wyatt, go up there and ask him some questions that might be helpful.

Wyatt points to the rectangle representing the picture and indicates that the picture is in the middle of the room. He asks Ethan if he is counting the entire length of the box (3 feet) or if he is counting from the middle of the picture to the end (1.5). By doing so, Wyatt asks Ethan to clarify his thinking.

Ethan explains his drawing by pointing out that each length of a square represents one foot. His 25 boxes represent 25 feet, which is the length of the room. He does not quite understand what Wyatt is asking. Brandon raises his hand and points out that he thinks that Ethan has accidentally not drawn the box in the center of the room. He points out that there are 12 boxes on the right hand side of the box. The teacher asks Brandon to go up there and explain what he means. Brandon walks to the interactive white board to share his observation.

> *Teacher:* So, how many feet have we used if we have 10 + 3 + 12? Do we get 25 feet?

Ethan looks as his drawing and changes his mind. After reflecting on Brandon's reasoning, Ethan reworks the problem and arrives at the correct answer.

Phase 3: Developing New Mathematical Insights. A discussion must lead to development of "big mathematical ideas" and skills that students can transfer to solve other problems. Therefore, at the end of the lesson the teacher and students should summarize what they learned. In Video Clip 1.4, students describe what they learned and strategies they can use to solve similar problems. In addition, they also report how to be successful math students. The students say that whole class discussions help them learn to persevere if they make a mistake, and the importance of checking work and being flexible. They share comments like "don't just give up, keep trying, check over your work, and keep trying until you get it right." Their comments, as listed below, show growth in understanding mathematical ideas, representations as an aid to learning, and a change in disposition, in which they see themselves as learners.

> The big idea is that you have to remember to find both sides. You have to . . . minus both sides. (*mathematical ideas*)

> Be really exact with drawings; make it straight. (*representations*)

> It is okay to get a wrong answer but don't be stuck with that and think you have the right answer. It is okay if you figure out a mistake on the board. It is always good to check your work after you figured it out. (*disposition*)

Video Clip 1.4 illustrates that communication takes many forms. The partner talk, the small group discussions, and the use of drawings as representations to support and communicate thinking all contributed to the whole class discussion. The students' comments illustrate that not only did they deepen their understanding of how to solve similar problems but they also developed skills needed to study mathematics.

SELF-REFLECTION QUESTIONS

1. What should the teacher's role in the discussion be?

2. How can you encourage students to do the thinking instead of relying on you for answers?

3. How can you use a range of students' answers to gauge their understanding?

When looking at these transcripts and the video, examine the nature of the conversation. What was discussed? How did this discussion take place? What was the teacher's role? What was the students' role? Did new mathematical understandings develop? Was there value in discussing these types of reasoning and issues as a whole class?

Additional Considerations for Facilitating Effective Discussions

Whole class discussions are much easier to facilitate if the physical space in the classroom has been set up for discussion. In addition, the teacher also needs to cultivate an appropriate social environment for discussion by establishing routines that make discussion easier. Chapter 2 provides ideas on how to set up the classroom space. Chapter 3 explains how to cultivate the social environment for discussion. For example, Ms. Bertolone-Smith and Ms. Malone actively work on creating a classroom culture for discussion. "We set up an environment where it is unacceptable for everyone not to participate." They want students to actively talk to each other, stay mentally engaged, and challenge each other's thinking during the math lesson. This expectation is strongly communicated to students. For example, the teachers actively work to make sure the conversations between partners/small groups are meaningful and challenging. If the students are not communicating effectively, they are moved to a different partner. In other words, the teachers maintain flexible groups all the time. Establishing a classroom environment for discussion requires active thought and development throughout the school year.

Chapter Summary

This book focuses on the type of communication covered in the Common Core State and NCTM standards. The purpose of the whole class discussion is to support students' developmental, conceptual, and procedural understanding of mathematics through problem solving, reasoning, communication, and sense-making. An effective discussion includes three phases: (1) making thinking explicit, (2) analyzing each other's solutions, and (3) developing new mathematical insights. Whole class discussions contribute to efficient use of class time to support student learning.

STUDY GUIDE

Below is a suggested sequence of activities designed to help you apply whole class discussions in your classroom and to think about how whole class discussions can support mathematical learning.

Examine Discussion Supported Mathematical Learning

1. Watch the Video Clips outlined in the chapter and review the *Reflecting on Video Clips* questions.
2. Think about how whole class discussion can support mathematical learning.
3. Read the Video Case Study on the next page.

Try Ideas Out!

1. Once you have thought about how whole class discussions support learning, try some of the ideas listed in *Strategies for Your Classroom.*
2. Complete the *Reflecting on Practice* worksheet. If you are a pre-service teacher, you can observe a classroom and use your observations to think about the questions provided in the *Reflecting on Practice* worksheet.

What Makes an Effective or Ineffective Discussion?

Reflect on what makes an effective and ineffective discussion. Thinking about your own classroom discussions and observations you have made while watching someone else's discussions are great places to begin thinking about what makes effective discussions. Consider the aspects of the *Reflecting on Practice* worksheet and the Video Clips to further examine how classroom discussion supports mathematical learning.

Tool Box: PDToolkit

- *Strategies for Your Classroom:* How and When to Use Whole Class Discussion to Support Learning
- Videos Clips 1.1, 1.2, 1.3, & 1.4
- *Reflecting on Video Clips*
- *Reflecting on Practice:* Using Whole Class Discussions
- PowerPoint: Chapter 1—Why Whole Class Discussions?

VIDEO CASE STUDY

Problem-Solving Using Schematic Drawings

Class: Grades 5 and 6 / **Teachers:** Ms. Bertolone-Smith and Ms. Malone

The Lesson

Ms. Claudia Bertolone-Smith and Ms. Marlene Malone team-teach math in a combined fifth and sixth grade class. They have approximately 57 students. Minden Elementary School, located in Nevada, is a Title 1 school. This video case shows Ms. Bertolone–Smith and Ms. Malone team-teaching a lesson based on students solving a rich, multi-step problem. The teaching objective is to have students use schematic drawings to support their thinking, and to make the use of schematic drawings part of the problem-solving process.

> **Problem 1:** A picture 3 feet across hangs in the center of a wall that is 25 feet long. How many feet from the left end of the wall is the left edge of the picture? (Kalman, 2008)*

Video Clip 1.4: Fifth & Sixth Grade Class: Problem-Solving Lesson   (0:13:52)

Before you watch Video Clip 1.4, solve Problem 1. This will help you follow the students' explanations. Think about how to represent the problem.

1. What strategies can be used to solve the problem?
2. What do you think students might do?
3. What misconceptions might students have?

Watch the video and think about the following questions:

1. Did the students gain new mathematical insights as a result of this discussion? Why or why not?
2. Did students make connections between each other's explanations? If so, how did this happen?
3. What caused the student to self-correct his answer?
4. Where in the video do each of the three different phases that are listed in Table 1.2 occur?
5. What was the role of the teacher?
6. How did the students participate in this discussion?
7. Did learning take place?

*Richard Kalman (Ed.). (2008). Math Olympiad Context Problem. Volume 2, p. 65. Problem 2A, Mathematical Olympiad for Elementary and Middle Schools INC. Bellmore, NY.

PD **pd** TOOLKIT™

How and When to Use Whole Class Discussion to Support Learning

Use whole class discussion to:

- Introduce new mathematical ideas
- Address misconceptions and errors
- Help students make deeper mathematical connections
- Help students develop more efficient strategies

Whole class discussion should:

- Focus on sense-making, reasoning and communication
- Build on small group and partner talk
- Address needs of diverse learners
- Help students develop new mathematical insights

CHAPTER 1

REFLECTING ON VIDEO CLIPS

Video Clip 1.1: Student Interview: Student Perspectives on "Math Talk" and Math Learning

1. What are these students' perspectives on how "math talk" helps them learn math?
2. What do these students say are the differences between partner talk and whole class discussion?
3. What kinds of experiences related to "math talk" have these students had in their math class?
4. What insights did you gain listening to these students talk about math?

Video Clip 1.2: Fifth & Sixth Grade Teacher Perspectives on Class Discussion

1. What are the teachers' mathematical goals for this lesson? Why did they choose these goals? How do these goals contribute to sense-making and discussion?
2. How did the teachers create the classroom environment for discussion with partners?
3. What are the teachers' perspectives about the value of using partner and small group discussions to teach math? Would you consider using different combinations of math talk in the classroom? Why or why not?
4. What are the teachers' perspectives on the role of whole class discussions as a means of supporting mathematical learning?

Video Clip 1.3: Fifth & Sixth Grade Teacher Interview on Lesson Planning

1. What are the teachers' perspectives on lesson planning?
2. What kinds of lessons promote high level thinking and discussion?
3. What insights did you gain as a result of watching this video?

Video Clip 1.4: Fifth & Sixth Grade Problem-Solving Lesson

Note: Before you watch Video Clip 1.4, solve Problem 1, found in the Video Case Study section. This will help you follow the students' explanations. Think about how to represent the problem.

1. What strategies can be used to solve the problem?
2. What do you think students might do?
3. What misconceptions might students have?

Now, watch the video and think about the following questions:

1. Did the students gain new mathematical insights as a result of this discussion? Why or why not?
2. Did students make connections between each other's explanations? If so, how did this happen?
3. What caused the student to self-correct his answer?
4. Where in the video do each of the three different phases that are listed in Table 1.2 occur?
5. What was the role of the teacher?
6. How did the students participate in this discussion?
7. Did learning take place?

REFLECTING ON PRACTICE

Using Whole Class Discussions

1. How do you use whole class discussions in your math lessons?

2. What plan is there for whole class discussions?

3. What are some challenges to implementing effective whole class discussions?

4. What are some of your areas of strengths and weaknesses in facilitating discussions?

5. What are some areas of facilitating discussions that you would like to work on?

Designing the Physical Classroom Space for Discussions

Best discussions take place where there is a spirit of inquiry and environment of trust.

(Spiegel, 2005)

As mentioned in Chapter 1, a well-designed classroom space enhances discussions. This chapter explores how to design the physical layout of the classroom and organize classroom spaces for both small group and whole class discussions. Students should be able to easily move to these locations and have access to the tools and resources they need for discussions. In the classroom shown below, students are seated on the floor and using their notebooks to record information about the problem they are working on. All the students can see the easel and teacher, which is one of the essential elements for designing a classroom that facilitates discussion.

Design Elements for Classroom Space

There are several essential classroom design elements to consider when setting up your classroom to facilitate whole class discussion. Organizing the classroom's physical space for effective discussions means creating a focal point, having a place for students and the teacher to gather comfortably, giving easy access to tools

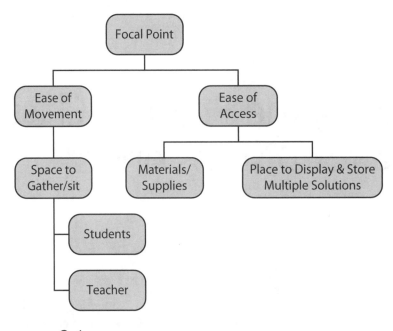

FIGURE **2.1**
Design elements for physical space for discussion

FIGURE **2.2**
A special carpeted area for whole class discussions

and materials needed during discussions, and reserving a space to display student work. These elements are illustrated in Figure 2.1 above.

It is important to visualize how these elements can be incorporated into an actual classroom. Figure 2.2 is an example of how one teacher organized her space for whole class discussion. Let's discuss how she uses the physical space of her classroom to implement the elements in Figure 2.1.

First, students are physically gathered together on the carpet, which is set up to clearly indicate that it is the designated space for whole class discussions. Students also bring their math journals to the carpet area so they can refer to the work from their partner or small group discussions when explaining or justifying their thinking. The whole class can see the easel, on which the teacher has written "$\frac{2}{3} = \frac{6}{9}$, true or false?" The teacher is seated behind the students where she can also see the focal point of the discussion. Notice that a student is moving forward to share her ideas about the concept of equivalent fractions and to explain that $\frac{2}{3}$ is equal to $\frac{6}{9}$. The other students listen intently to her explanation. Another student has already written his explanation on the chart paper that is on the easel. You can see the chart paper from the previous day's discussion is displayed on the bulletin board next to the easel.

The way that the space is organized influences the kinds of interactions that can take place during a discussion. The chart paper easel creates a focal point for students to look at during the conversation. The carpet space becomes an intimate setting for students to gather together. The chart paper on the board displaying student work makes it possible to refer to previous discussions and solutions. Once the physical space is prepared, it is important to make sure that it is functional as well as comfortable.

SELF-REFLECTION QUESTION

How does the space in your classroom contribute to small group and whole class discussions?

Designing a Functional Space for Discussions

At the beginning of the school year, teachers prepare their classrooms by making decisions about the arrangement of student desks, the teacher desk, materials, and the use of space for activities and meetings. Decisions are influenced by the size of the room, the number of students, and the furniture available.

In addition to creating a warm and inviting environment, teachers need to consider the *functionality* of the space. Functionality involves thinking about how the space is going to be used for the variety of work the class will be doing. One of the most important things to consider is how students can move from space to space to get their work done. Because students will work in small groups, there must be spaces for them to meet, such as the

FIGURE 2.3
Space for small group discussions

table shown in Figure 2.3. In addition, students must be able to easily move from their small groups to a designated space for whole class discussions. Classroom transitions become smoother if the space is arranged so that students can efficiently navigate from one space and activity to the other. Take into consideration the ease of access students have to tools and resources they will use to communicate in the various spaces. Once the space is organized, students will be able to familiarize themselves with which spaces are designated for certain types of activities and how to quickly navigate the physical space between small group discussion and whole class discussion.

Designing Space for Small Group Discussion

When small groups gather, they need a common work space that allows them to face each other. Being face to face makes it easier for them to communicate. Students also need to have access to the tools and resources needed for the lesson. You can either group individual desks together so that students face each other, or use larger desks that can seat several students. Make sure that you are able to walk around the groups to monitor the discussions and observe students. You will use these observations to plan your whole class discussion.

Designing a Functional Space for Whole Class Discussions

Design elements that create a functional space for whole class discussions include a focal point, seating arrangements without distractions, and access to tools and materials. As discussed earlier, use available space to create a separate area for whole class discussions. Students (particularly younger students) are more focused on the discussion if they are physically gathered close together. This minimizes distractions and makes it easier to make eye contact. Close proximity also helps teachers observe students' facial expressions and body language. These are important physical cues that identify which students are engaged in the discussion, which students are confused, and which students are truly grasping the lesson.

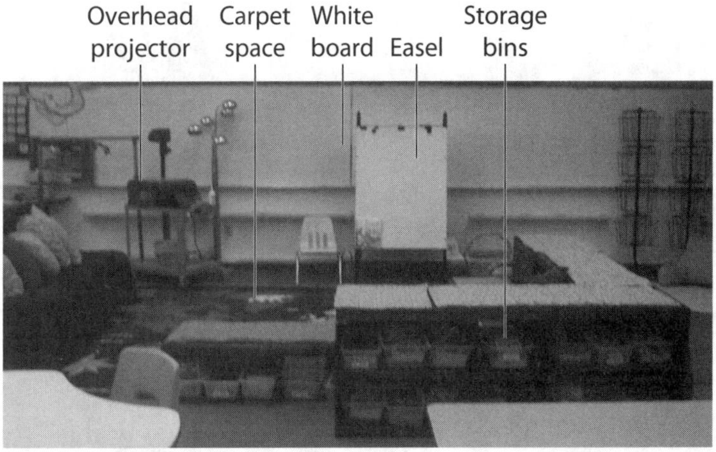

Figure 2.4 provides an example of how one teacher has organized her classroom space for whole class discussions. The teacher used an area rug to create a separate space for whole class discussion. The rug is placed in front of the white board, between extra seating and storage units. This arrangement clearly structures where students sit for whole class discussion by offering extra definition to the discussion area. Placing a chart paper easel in front of the white boards allows the students to use the chart paper easel and the white board space as needed. In addition, an overhead projector is also available close to the focal point, which gives the teacher easy access to another teaching tool without moving away from the focal point.

Overhead projector Carpet space White board Easel Storage bins

FIGURE 2.4
Organized space for whole class discussion

Creating a Focal Point

A *focal point* is the part of the whole group discussion area at which students will be looking during the whole class discussion, as pictured in Figure 2.5. Because the focal point needs to be the center of their attention, it is imperative that all the students can see what is being demonstrated from where they are sitting. The focal point can be a chart paper easel or a white board, but it must be something on which the students can write as they participate in the discussion. The focal point is so important because it is where students will demonstrate their thinking and make comparisons between multiple representations of the problem they are solving. If a student writes a solution to a problem that some students can't see, the visual representation becomes a useless tool for discussion.

To encourage students to answer questions through discussion, the focal point needs to be the easel or white board, not the teacher. Researchers Nathan

FIGURE **2.5**
Creating a focal point for discussion helps focus attention and discussion

& Knuth (2003) found that when the teacher physically removes herself from the focal point and asks questions from the back of the group, the students begin to talk to each other rather than talking directly to the teacher. Students are often willing to take ownership of the conversation when the teacher is not the center of the conversation. However, the topic may require the teacher to stand in front of the group to discuss or scaffold ideas, particularly if the subject is challenging or the discussion is slow to start. Therefore, teachers need to be able to move easily to and from the focal point as needed.

Teachers also need to be able to quickly evaluate the best place to stand for each class. Part of that decision will depend on how dependent the discussion is on the teacher participating in the visual representation of the lesson.

SELF-REFLECTION QUESTIONS

1. Where do you usually stand during a classroom lesson?

2. When should you remove yourself from the center to allow students to engage in conversation with each other?

Visualization and Representations

Visualization is the ability to form a mental image of an idea or concept. In mathematics, it can be hard to understand what another person is thinking and explaining. However, if students use a model or draw a diagram to support an explanation, it is easier to understand their reasoning. According to the NCTM *Principles and Standards for School Mathematics* (2000), representations such as diagrams, graphical displays, and symbolic expressions are an integral part of communication and sense-making.

When a student demonstrates thinking through drawings, pointing, or explanations, it is easier for both the teacher and the other students to visualize and understand the student's explanation. For example, to figure out how to a divide a pizza into fourths, a student might draw a circle and say "I first drew a line like this, and then I did it again like this and then I got 4 pieces." During the whole class discussion, the student must explain that the circle represents a pizza and the lines represent his divisions to attribute meaning to the representation.

Access to Materials for Students' Work

Students can use physical tools to represent their ideas and communicate their thinking (NCTM, 2000). In the previous example, the student would need a marker and an easel or white board to draw his "pizza" and divide it. Students need manipulatives, pens, paper, and access to chart paper or a dry erase board. Making these materials accessible near the focal point ensures that the flow of the classroom discussion is not interrupted by students or the teacher leaving the discussion area to retrieve needed materials.

The shelves in Figure 2.6 contain many different kinds of materials that are easily accessible to the teacher and students. By using clear containers, students can quickly see what kinds of tools are available and know where to return them after discussion. To ensure good discussion ettiquette, give students easy access to general discussion guidelines and key vocabulary by hanging the information where everyone can see it from the discussion area.

Access to Technology

Technology such as LCD projectors, interactive white boards, document cameras, class websites, and other computer software enhances teaching and learning mathematics by providing students with representations that are difficult to do by hand (NCTM, 2000). Technology can be effectively integrated as part of discussions if it is located within the focal

FIGURE 2.6

Easily accessible materials for student use during discussions point or easily accessible during the discussion. Technology may eliminate the need to create and store chart paper records. For example, student work can be displayed in a document camera and saved for later use. Students can write on the interactive white board that displays other students' work to add their thoughts without actually marking the original work. If you have an interactive white board with a document camera, make sure the camera is easily accessible close to the focal point so that students don't have to travel to a different section of the classroom to retreive it.

Displaying and Saving Students' Work

We have discussed that it is important to save student work from class discussions, and there are several reasons to do so. Saving student work and having it accessible allows students to return and reference various problem-solving skills, which encourages them to try and apply many concepts when faced with a challenging problem.

Class length is another reason to have a system for saving and displaying student work. If the bell rings before you have finished your whole class discussion, student work should be saved so that it can be easily accessed the next day. One teacher uses a clothes rack with pants hangers to save the work students have done on chart paper, as illustrated in Figure 2.7. Students can access the coat rack during small group discussion, whole class discussion, or seat work. Easy access to previously created ideas allows discussions to continue smoothly.

Unfortunately, this easy access to earlier work is not the norm. More often, students immediately erase their drawings after they explain their thinking during whole class discussions. Consequently, erasing work prevents students from making comparisons between each other's ideas or revisiting ideas. Storage systems like

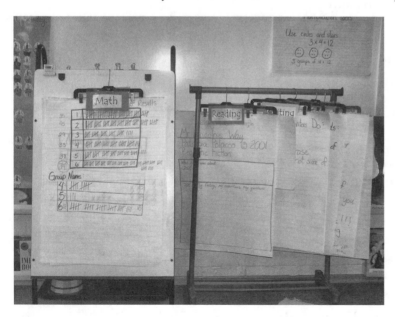

FIGURE 2.7

(left) An easel displays student work as it is being discussed.
(Right) A coat rack stores work nearby for future reference.

the clothes rack are advantageous because they are space-friendly, easily accessible, store several classes worth of material, and can be moved as needed. Interactive smart boards can be used to save work as well, and don't have the same physical limitations as chart paper storage systems.

Further Suggestions for Classroom Layouts

The diagrams in Figure 2.8 provide examples of classroom arrangements that facilitate whole class discussions. The large rectangle in Figure 2.8a and large circle in Figure 2.8b represent carpeted areas. In all three diagrams, there is a clear focal point. Figures 2.8a and b show classrooms with separate carpet space and focal point for discussion. Teachers have reported that a separate carpet space helps students stay focused because distractions are minimized. However, if the students are older and there is limited classroom space, furniture could be arranged so that students can face the focal point with minimal distractions, as shown in Figure 2.8c.

Classrooms often begin the year with a well-designed space. However, material accumulates as the year progresses, and the space becomes disorganized. Therefore, no matter how the physical layout of the classroom is designed, space must periodically be examined and de-cluttered in order to maintain an efficient classroom.

a.
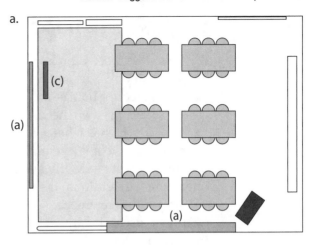

b.
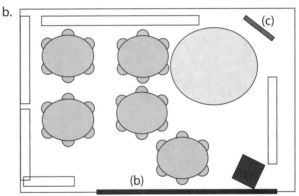

c.
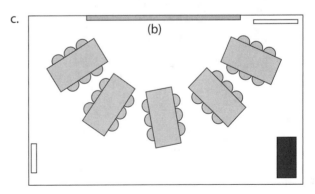

(a) White board   (b) Interactive white board   (c) Easel

FIGURE 2.8

Arrangements of classroom space for whole class discussions

Chapter Summary

A whole class discussion is much easier to facilitate when the physical space of the classroom is designed with discussions in mind. The classroom needs to be designed for both small group and whole class discussion. For whole class discussions, there needs to be space for students to gather around the focal point, which is where students look during the discussion to display their work and to analyze multiple representations. Materials and tools for discussion must be readily available so that the flow of conversation is not interrupted. In addition, the teacher must think about how to save student work for future reference. A well-designed physical space optimizes the quality of discussion by saving time and contributing to a smooth flow of the conversation.

STUDY GUIDE

Below is a suggested sequence of activities designed to help you organize your classroom in a way that optimizes your classroom space for discussions.

Design Optimal Classroom Space for Discussions

1. Evaluate and explore the design features of your own classroom.
2. Think about how to design your classroom even if you are not teaching yet.

Practicing Teacher

1. Review the *Strategies for Your Classroom: Considerations for Creating Physical Space*. If you have your own classroom, evaluate the layout. Think about the design of your classroom for both small group and whole class discussions. Specifically examine functionality of your space for movement, displaying work, and having access to tools needed during math discussions.

2. Use the *Physical Layouts for Classroom Discussion Checklist* to guide you while you examine your space for design and functionality that facilitates discussions.

3. Ask a colleague for feedback on your redesigned space. It is helpful to give your colleague a blank copy of *Physical Layouts for Classroom Discussion Checklist*. It will guide them to review your changes in a more concrete way. Having another person evaluate your space may give you a fresh perspective or a layout idea you overlooked.

Pre-Service Teacher

1. If you do not have your classroom just yet, try to imagine how you would like to organize your space. You can also use classrooms you have observed in the past, and think about how you would modify that organization based on the *Physical Layouts for Classroom Discussion Checklist*.

2. Draw a diagram of your room on the *Reflecting on Practice* worksheet.

3. Have peers evaluate your layout. It may helpful to give your colleague a blank copy of *Physical Layouts for Classroom Discussion Checklist*. Using these tools offers an opportunity for further discussion of classroom types and layout options that could optimize whole class discussion.

Tool Box: PDToolkit

- *Strategies for Your Classroom:* Considerations for Creating Physical Space
- *Reflecting on Practice:* Designing Classroom Space
- *Physical Layouts for Classroom Discussions Checklist*
- PowerPoint: Chapter 2—Designing the Physical Classroom Space for Discussion

Considerations for Creating Physical Space

Small Group Discussion Space

- Create a common space to work where students can see each other
- Have space for the teacher to walk around and observe student conversations
- Set clear paths for students to transition to the whole group space (such as a carpet)

Large Group Discussion Space

- Implement a point that can be viewed by all students (e.g., white board, interactive board, easel with chart paper)
- Reserve a place to display multiple student work
- Designate space for students to sit facing the focal point
- Clear a path for students to walk back and forth to the focal point while sharing answers
- Have a place for the teacher to stand both in front of and behind the group during the discussion
- Create a storage place for materials and supplies that is close to the focal point
- Have access to technology (e.g., doc cam and interactive boards)
- Create a system for storing student work for future reference (either physically or digitally)

REFLECTING ON PRACTICE

Designing Classroom Space

1. Draw a diagram of how you would organize your classroom space.

2. Describe the *functional* features of your space.

   _____

   _____

   _____

   _____

   _____

3. What technology and tools do you have available in your class for discussion? Are they located in a place with easy access during the discussion?

   _____

   _____

   _____

   _____

   _____

   _____

   _____

   _____

   _____

Physical Layouts for Classroom Discussions Checklist

Use this checklist to evaluate the design and functionality of your classroom space for discussions. Once you have made your changes, ask a colleague or math coach to provide you with their impressions.

	Observed	Notes—To-do list
Small Group		
Is there space for small group discussion?		
Is there space for the teacher to walk around and observe the students?		
Are there paths for students to walk to the whole group space?		
Whole Group		
Is the focal point visible to the whole group?		
Does the focal point have a place to write ideas and representations?		
Is there a place for students to sit?		
Is there a place for the teacher to stand/sit both in front of and away from the focal point?		
Do you have access to technology for discussions?		
Do you have easy access to materials and supplies for discussion?		
Is there a place to share multiple student work?		
Do you have a place to store student work (either physically or digitally)?		
Overall Effectiveness		
Areas that need improvement		
Areas that need de-cluttering		

Developing Classroom Routines for Whole Class Discussions

Effective teachers have invisible procedures. Observers in the classroom don't see them, but they know they exist. That is why effective teachers' classrooms run so smoothly.

(Wong & Wong, 2009, p. 195)

The classroom social environment can either stimulate productive discussions or stifle thinking and sharing ideas. How students interact with each other and the teacher matters. Students who are encouraged to participate freely in thought-provoking whole class discussions will share their ideas and opinions, challenge each other's thinking, and help the whole class develop mathematical insights. Before they are willing to be part of a discussion, students need to feel comfortable in the classroom. Therefore, the teacher needs to create a supportive *classroom community* that will facilitate productive discussions. Within this classroom community, physical and social routines for classroom discussion are developed to help students gain a deeper understanding of mathematical concepts.

Building a Supportive Classroom Community

In a classroom community, students feel connected to each other and trust each other. They work together for the common good to support their own learning as well as their peers (Hardin, 2011). Patrick, Turner, Meyer & Midgley (2003) discovered that students who felt emotionally and intellectually supported performed better in mathematics and engaged in class discussions. In contrast, they discovered that students who did not feel supported used "avoidance tactics" when it was time to do math. Therefore, Patrick, et al. (2003) concluded that teachers who create supportive environments are more successful in involving students in math discussion than teachers who do not focus on building supportive environments. They found that teachers connected with students and built supportive learning environments by using humor, revealing something personal about themselves, showing respect for students, sharing enthusiasm for learning mathematics, and voicing expectations that all students can learn (Patrick, Turner, Meyer & Midgley, 2003). Building a classroom learning community aids classroom management because the teacher must create classroom rituals, allow students to get to know each other, and promote kindness and caring (Larrivee, 2008).

Not only does the teacher's interaction with students matter, but how classmates treat each other also makes a difference. When students feel threatened, they do not share their ideas (Jenson, 2008). They don't like to feel criticized and judged on their abilities. Students need to see themselves as helping each other as opposed to criticizing and assessing each other. Jenson found that students who felt uncomfortable gave "step by step" procedural answers instead of sharing their reasoning processes on how they solved the problem.

A good first step to show students your commitment to a classroom community is to discuss building a classroom community at the beginning of the school year. Impress on students that they are all part of a learning community and their goal as students is to learn from and support each other. From your first class, it is important to set the stage for how you interact with your students. The next sections will cover some ways to get started:

1. Connect with the students through mutual respect.
2. Value students' experiences and home language.
3. Assign students to work with different partners or small groups so that students get the opportunity to know each other.

Establish Mutual Respect

A teacher who maintains positive interaction with students by showing respect and caring facilitates the development of a classroom community (Hardin, 2011).

A Peek Inside the Classroom

In Video Clip 3.1, Student Interview: Cultivating a Classroom Community, students in Ms. Bertolone-Smith and Ms. Moyer's class express how important it is for them to feel comfortable enough to share with each other and to seek help when stuck. Students point out that the teachers make them feel comfortable by using humor:

Video Clip 3.1 Student Interview: Cultivating a Classroom Community (0:1:50)

> "They make something funny, like they just don't say go in this book and do whatever."

> "Yeah, some teachers are so textbook, but Ms. Moyer and Ms. B always joke and they are always so fun with us. It is like we want to be building a community and having fun with each other."

> "At the beginning of year, there were some kids who were shy and [said] 'I don't really want to be out there' and then Ms. Moyer and Ms. B will teach you how to get out there and by the end of the year they are all crazy just like the rest of the class."

PD **TOOLKIT**™

for *Whole Class Mathematics Discussions*

View the video online at PDToolkit.

Students' comments reveal that the way their teacher interacts with them influences their ability to feel like a part of a community. Even the students understand that at the beginning of the year some of their peers felt uncomfortable sharing their ideas. The teacher had to give these students strategies for participating in discussions and to help build the classroom community. Learning to share ideas with their peers was important from the students' perspective.

Value Students' Experiences and Home Language

Placing value on informal home language and cultural experiences helps students make connections between their everyday experiences, language, and formal mathematics (National Research Council, 2001). Children also should be encouraged to communicate with their families about the mathematics they are learning, which helps children develop both descriptive language and conventional vocabulary (Whitin & Whitin, 2002).

The following fifth-grade math lesson covering fractions and units exemplifies how valuing student experiences and home language facilitates math discussion and deepens student understanding of the math concepts from the lesson.

Fifth-grade students were given the task of planning a party for twenty children. Part of the planning involved choosing food to serve at the party. This assignment led to discussions about the foods that students liked to eat and how different families celebrated events. After students listed the food items they wanted to serve at the party, they investigated how much of each item they needed to buy. The decision to purchase several six-packs of soda led to a whole class discussion on units.

When students discussed the kinds of foods that they liked, they were sharing their home and cultural experiences using informal language. Through this cultural discussion, students were able to learn about each other as individuals. They also were able to apply the math lesson and practice communicating the concept in class. This practice enables students to share their math learning with their families later.

Use Small Groups/Partners

Although students can form close friendships when they work with the same classmates in a small group throughout the year, they may not feel comfortable with the rest of the class, which can hinder whole class discussion. Therefore, students need opportunities to interact with all their classmates to help them get to know each other and to experience different perspectives. Changing partners and groups increases the comfort level of the class and contributes to a nonthreatening classroom environment that supports discussions.

Small groups contribute to class discussion in other ways too. When students work in small groups, they can get help from peers, clarify their thinking, and express their ideas more freely than they can in whole class discussions. After students have articulated their ideas and listened to others, they have more to contribute to the whole class discussion.

A Peek Inside the Classroom

In Video Clip 3.2, Fifth & Sixth Grade Teacher Interview: Using Flexible Grouping, teachers explain how they use flexible groups or partners to set up an environment in which nonparticipation is considered unacceptable.

PD **TOOLKIT**™

for *Whole Class Mathematics Discussions*

View the video online at PDToolkit.

Video Clip 3.2 Fifth & Sixth Grade Teacher Interview: Using Flexible Grouping (00:03:07)

41

Physical
Classroom
Routines
to Prepare
for Whole Class
Discussions

Ms. Moyer says, "We feel like we set up an environment where it is unacceptable not to participate. So we do a few things in order to 'force it' and create that environment. One of them is [using] flexible groups all the time." Ms. Bertolone-Smith establishes the expectation that students must be discussing mathematics when they are working in groups by making physical changes to the groups. She listens to each group's conversations and moves students around if the conversations are not related to the math discussion or the student chemistry is off, both of which are detrimental to preparing for whole class discussion.

Physical Classroom Routines to Prepare for Whole Class Discussions

Routines are necessary for classrooms to function effectively and to set expectations for students' behavior (Hardin, 2011). Classroom routines must be *simple* and *consistent* so that students know what to expect. These routines should be introduced at the beginning of the school year and regularly revisited and refined.

Students need *physical routines* to prepare for the discussion and effectively communicate their ideas (Cobb, Yackel, & McClain, 2000). Physical routines can aid classroom management and save time. To prepare for and to participate in the discussion, students need to know when a discussion is going to take place, where to sit, and what supplies are needed. In addition, they need to physically demonstrate that they are ready to engage in the discussion.

A signal can let the students know that it is time to mentally and physically get ready for a discussion. For example, the teacher can signal discussion time by ringing a bell. Students will need to know what physical procedure to follow to prepare for discussion. Some teachers designate carpet space or another area for discussions and assign students a special spot where they can sit. Knowing that, students will move to their assigned space when the bell rings. Teachers also need to let students know what physical objects they will need to participate in discussion. Some teachers may incorporate collecting items (such as math manipulatives) into walking to the discussion area. If the materials are in the discussion area, a teacher might say, "I want you to place the math manipulatives in front of you." The goal is to minimize distractions so that students focus their attention on the discussion.

A teacher can ask students if they are physically ready for the discussion by saying, "Show me that you are ready to participate in the discussion. I know you are ready to listen and share ideas when you are quiet and looking at me."

SELF-REFLECTION QUESTION

What physical routines have you established in your class in order to prepare for whole class discussions?

Strategies and Social Routines for Whole Class Discussions

The purpose of a whole class discussion is to explore mathematical concepts or problems as a class. Discussions support learning because they involve more than students simply sharing answers. Instead, students must dig deeper, and test out new theories in order to develop new insights. How students communicate and interact with each other influences the mathematical understandings they develop (Boaler, 1997; Boaler & Greeno, 2000; Hiebert et al., 1997; Schoenfeld, 1998). Students have to engage in problem solving, communicate their thinking with others, listen to alternate views, and reflect on their solutions.

Discussions engage students in sense-making. When students must explain their reasoning, they clarify their own thoughts; learning takes place as they voice their ideas. The other students think about the facts presented and develop a shared understanding of the explanation so that the subsequent conversation can build on each other's ideas. Therefore, effective communication involves making sure everyone in the group understands the reasoning presented.

The ultimate goal of the discussions is for students to develop a deep conceptual understanding of mathematics and efficient problem-solving strategies. When students have to think about their solutions and reflect on their thinking in order to communicate to others, they are engaging in *metacognition*. Metacognition is needed for learning to take place (National Research Council, 2001). Furthermore, understanding *how* and *why* something works is an important part of how people learn. A student who explains the solution to a problem step by step is providing a "calculational" explanation (Yackel & Cobb, 1996). A student who can explain and justify how and why something works has processed the mathematics at a deeper conceptual level. However, both kinds of explanations are necessary in whole class discussions in order for mathematical learning to take place (Yackel & Cobb, 1996; Star, 2005 & Baroody, Feil, & Johnson, 2007). Students not only need to have a rich understanding of how concepts are interrelated, they should also understand how to use algorithms accurately to solve problems (Star, 2005; Baroody, et al., 2007).

If students' prior math discussion experiences involve mainly calculational explanations or performing calculations to get the correct answer, students may initially resist new expectations requiring them to explain their thought processes and why something works (Cobb, Stephan, McClain, & Gravemeijer, 2001). Being asked to explain their reasoning and approaches to solving problems may challenge students' comfort level. Some teachers report that students "don't like to talk." However, their resistance can be overcome when (1) the teacher sets clear expectations that students should prepare for and participate in the discussion, (2) the teacher establishes routines that require students to share their ideas and justify their strategies for solving problems, and (3) the class practices these routines daily. One teacher reported that when she first started implementing these strategies for discussion, her students' initial test scores dropped slightly. (Her district administered a test that measured student growth during the school year.) However, she continued to apply the strategies in this book for whole class discussion, and at the end of the school year her students had the highest growth in test scores. Therefore, be patient if students initially resist new expectations and routines. Consistently apply them and students will start opening up more during the discussion.

For more detailed examination of whole class discussions, review the case studies on pages 49–51. Case Study 1 analyzes an ineffective whole class discussion. Case Study 2 demonstrates how the same teacher effectively changed her whole class discussion style to support her students as conceptually explored mathematics.

Routines for Communication

The key to success is using routines for communication consistently and ensuring that students understand the purpose of communication routines. Students have to be encouraged to communicate ideas clearly so that others can understand their reasoning; to listen, understand, and analyze another person's point of view; and to reflect on their own thinking.

Activate Prior Knowledge. Learning occurs when students connect new information with what they already know (National Research Council, 2001). When students activate their prior knowledge and think about a problem before the whole class discussion, they are likely to provide more meaningful contributions to the discussion. In addition, they may find it easier to follow and make sense of their peers' explanations.

Establish Expectations of Participation in Discussions. Students need to know ahead of time that they will be asked to share their thinking with others. This forces students to reflect on the problem more deeply. The following example illustrates how one teacher established expectations.

> Today you are going to get some problems. I would like you to work independently on the problem first. . . . When you are finished, I am going to assign you to work in small groups. Discuss and share your ideas about how to solve the problem. Then we will meet back as a class, and each group will share what they decided. You may solve the problems any way you like.

Allow Students Time to Think Before Sharing. Students must be given time to think about how to solve the problem before they start discussing their ideas. By first thinking about a problem and formulating possible solutions, students will be able to support and challenge thinking of other students.

Posing questions to guide thinking can require students to think more deeply about the problem they are trying to solve. After students have individually thought about the problem, they can work with partners or small group to try out ideas with each other before sharing with the whole class.

Communicating and Listening During Whole Class Discussions

Students need to understand that they are sharing their ideas so that other students can understand their thinking. Students must listen and ask questions if they are unclear about the explanation being presented. Model how to share ideas by using representations, stopping to make sure that students are following along, and asking questions to check comprehension.

Student explanations must be valued by the group (Bochicchio, Cole, Ostien, Rodriguez, Staples, Susla, & Truxaw, 2009). Researchers (Bochicchio et al.) point out that students feel comfortable sharing their ideas and opinions with the class only if they feel that their thoughts are valued. Students feel that their thoughts are valued when other students listen to what they are saying and provide constructive feedback on the ideas without criticizing the individual. Make a distinction between personal criticism and criticism about mathematical ideas. A critique of an idea is not a personal attack. The goal of the conversation is to understand what a student is saying. Therefore, if a student presents an incorrect argument or demonstrates a misconception, the class should view this as a learning opportunity to deepen their understanding of why something does not work.

Explain that disagreements will occur and that students will have different ways of thinking about problems. Asking higher-level questions can also prompt students' critical thinking. For example, you may ask students to justify their answers and explain why one answer works better than another. Provide guidelines on how to respectfully agree or disagree with a student's explanation. For example, students can say, "I agree (disagree) with Scott's strategy because. . . ." Students must justify why they agree or disagree with part or all of another student's reasoning, being clear that they are critiquing ideas and not criticizing individuals. Setting clear guidelines will help develop the community environment and encourage less confident students to participate in whole class discussions.

Active Listening During Whole Class Discussions

Active listening is an important part of sense-making in whole class discussions. Students should not passively sit and tune out of the discussion because it is not their turn to talk. The whole class should be listening to other students' explanations and thinking about the problem (Yackel, 2003). A teacher can ask students to model what "listening" physically looks like. In the following example, a teacher tells her students what she expects them to do during discussion.

> *Teacher:* I have some rules about how we have a conversation. . . .
> I want each person to talk out and explain their strategy. Every member needs to be listening because I am going to have you explain it later. For example, if I went over to Shawn and asked him how Carmen solved it, then Shawn should be able to tell me the way Carmen explained it. When it comes to your turn, you can say "I used Samantha's method" or "I used Carmen's method." Or, if you did something different, then you could say, "I used Amber's method but I did it this way."

The teacher clearly points out her expectations for students to participate in the discussion and communicate their ideas. She asks students to listen to each other's explanations. Students are expected to restate another student's explanation using that student's own words. Students also must connect their explanations with other students' thinking. Having other students contribute to another student's explanation or restating in a different way can help the class understand the solution or strategy. The teacher clearly establishes a purpose for listening and communicating as a group and models an enthusiasm for mathematical thinking.

Teachers also need to listen to the student explanations in order to determine what sense the students are making, what they conceptually understand, and what misconceptions they may have (Yackel, 2003). Use this information to facilitate and scaffold the discussion.

Inviting students to restate what another student has said or share a similar or different strategy will force students to compare their own strategy with the one being discussed.

Students need explicit instruction in routines for active listening and guidelines for acceptable peer interaction. Post class guidelines on how to listen and critically think about the ideas being shared on a bulletin board close to the focal point to remind students of behavior expectations. Suggestions for active listening are given on the *Strategies for Your Classroom* worksheet, under the section titled Routines for Active Listening and Making New Connections.

SELF-REFLECTION QUESTIONS

1. What routines do you currently have in place for communication?

2. How effectively do these routines support communication?

Using Representations to Record Thinking

The National Council of Teachers of Mathematics has an entire process standard devoted to representations. According to NCTM, students use representations to draw pictures, make diagrams, and use manipulatives when they are thinking through a problem. In addition to helping students think about the problem, representations are also helpful for communicating thinking to others.

Create, Share, and Explain Representations

When students create a representation to communicate their thinking, other students are able to visualize what they are saying. Video Clip 3.3 demonstrates how Ms. Rivara's second-grade students create a representation of their shoe size and use the cutout to measure the length and width of a table. During the whole class discussion, Ms. Rivara creates a chart to record the range of student measurements of the table. The chart enables students to view and compare the different measurements they made; without the chart, it would have been much harder for students to compare numbers. Students also used the cutouts of their shoes to compare lengths and explain their thinking. Creating, sharing, and explaining representations are an important part of classroom routines for discussion.

Students who are taught to solve problems by using algorithms may be resistant to drawing pictures and using representations. However, when students learn the algorithm without understanding how and why it works, they have difficulty retaining what they learned. Students may also lack number sense, which is needed to solve problems with algorithms. Students need to learn the "big ideas" of mathematics conceptually and then understand how and why an algorithm works. Using representations can help students develop number sense. For example, consider the problem 200 + 250. One student can solve it by adding 200 + 200 to make 400, then adding 50. Another student might recognize that 250 + 250 equals 500, and then subtract 50. Having flexible ways to think about a problem involves developing number sense. Flexibility leads to a deeper understanding of mathematics, and students are able to use problem-solving strategies if they forget particular steps for an algorithm. Encourage students to use representations to support their thinking and they will grasp larger concepts.

Using Representations to Connect to Another Student's Method

Students can make connections between their ideas and those of their peers by analyzing representations. For example, in Video Clip 3.3, Second Grade Measurement Lesson and Teacher Interview, Ms. Rivara poses a question that requires students to analyze and make sense of the data they collected when they used their cutouts to measure the table. Students must consider their own measurements and connect them to other students' measurements in order to answer the question.

PD **TOOLKIT**™

for *Whole Class Mathematics Discussions*

View the video online at PDToolkit.

A Peek Inside the Classroom

Watch in the video as students use their representations to explain their thinking.

> *Ms. Rivara:* Are your numbers the same? You all measured the same length, the long side and the small side. Are the numbers the same?
>
> *Students:* No.
>
> *Ms. Rivara:* Why not? Patrick, what do you think?
>
> *Patrick:* Because people have different feet. They are big or tiny.
>
> *Ms. Rivara:* Big or tiny, why would that matter?

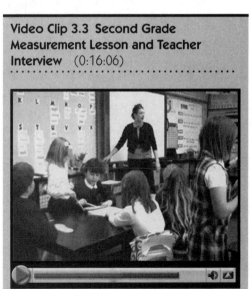

Video Clip 3.3 Second Grade Measurement Lesson and Teacher Interview (0:16:06)

Patrick's answer represents his observation that the chart contains the various measurements of the length and width of the table. He notices that the numbers in the chart are not the same. Ms. Rivara asks students to think about why it matters that the numbers were not the same.

> *Kayla:* Some people at the table have smaller feet than you, and others have bigger feet than you . . .

> *Ms. Rivara:* So, why would that matter? Would a smaller shoe measure more times? . . . We have 11 feet, 6 feet, or 7 feet. What is going on? What does it matter, depending on the size of your foot? Drew?

> *Drew:* Because the bigger feet, takes [a shorter] amount of feet to get to to the other side.

Ms. Rivara holds up two paper models representing two different shoe sizes, one behind the other, to illustrate that one is longer. Drew makes the connection between the numbers recorded in the chart, the representation of the shoe, and the actual shoe sizes. He is comparing the measurement he made for length with the measurements that other students made. Students are able to see that it takes fewer feet to measure the length or width of the table with a larger shoe size or if the unit of measurement is larger. The measurements in the chart, along with the paper representations, allow the conversation to shift from looking at numbers in the chart to evaluating what these numbers mean in relation to shoe sizes and measuring of the table. The class reaches the following understanding about nonstandard units:

- Each student has different size shoes.
- Longer length of the shoe yields a smaller measurement.
- Everyone will not get the same measurement using nonstandard units.

When students analyze representations, it is easier to understand how others are thinking. Furthermore, representations help students make mathematical connections to answer questions such as "What is a standard unit?" Analyzing representations and making connections should become part of the classroom routine for discussion.

SELF-REFLECTION QUESTIONS

1. How would you encourage students to use a variety of representations such as drawings and manipulatives when solving problems?

2. How do representations help whole class discussions?

Case Study 1: Examining an Unsuccessful Discussion

In the following case study, a teacher attempts to hold a whole class discussion about division, fractions, and decimals. The discussion is not built around recommended routines that would engage students in thinking about and sharing their ideas. As a result, a full discussion does not take place, and the teacher reverts to showing students step by step how to solve the problem. She concludes in her journal that these students "don't know how to express their ideas about math." As a result, she decides that she needs to "show students several strategies on how to solve problems."

SCENARIO: The teacher is standing in front of the overhead and the students are seated in rows facing the teacher. The students have their textbooks open to a page on decimals and fractions and their homework is also on their desks. The teacher wants her students to think about the relationship between division and fractions so she can relate it to the concept of decimals. Her specific lesson goal is to show students how to compare fractions by converting them to decimals and using the decimals to figure out which fraction is larger.

> *Teacher:* What does it means to divide?
>
> *Student:* Dividing by an angle?
>
> *Student:* Decimals and fractions?

ANALYSIS: The teacher starts with a good question with the potential for students to dig deeper to understand the meaning of division. However, she does not begin with a problem that would require students to think about division. The student who responded "decimals and fractions" is likely making a prediction based on the fact that the textbook is open to a page with that lesson title.

> *Teacher:* Who likes decimals and fractions? Are decimals and fractions the same?
>
> *Students:* Yes.

ANALYSIS: Although several students agree that decimals and fractions are the same, they offer no explanation. This question has also shifted focus of the original

continues on next page

Case Study, continued

question of "what it means to divide." Now, students are trying to decide if decimals and fractions are the same and if they like fractions and decimals.

> *Teacher:* Let's compare fractions. What's greater? Raise your hands. I want you to think about it. How can we compare two fractions? What is the greater fraction, ¾ or 6⁄7?
>
> *Student:* 6⁄7.
>
> *Teacher:* Okay, I want you to think about it. Raise your hand. How many think ¾ is greater? Raise your hand if you think 6⁄7 is greater. How many are not sure? What can we do to compare the two fractions?

ANALYSIS: Although the teacher is asking students to decide if "¾ is bigger than 6⁄7," her goal is to help students understand that they can convert the fractions to decimals and then compare the numbers. The focus is on finding the correct answer as opposed to helping students figure out conceptually how to compare fractions. The students still seem to be struggling; the teacher decides to show them how to find the common denominator. She asks students to multiply the numbers as she solves the problem.

> *Teacher:* Can we write them both as fractions with 28 as a denominator? Could we do that? What is four times six?
>
> *Students:* Twenty-four.
>
> *Teacher:* What is seven times three?
>
> *Students:* Twenty-one.
>
> *Teacher:* How does twenty-one compare to twenty-four?
>
> *Students:* It is smaller.
>
> *Teacher:* So, which fraction is greater?
>
> *Students:* 6⁄7.

ANALYSIS: Students are able to answer her questions because they involve calculations that they can do. However, it is unclear if they understand why 6⁄7 is greater than ¾, and if they could solve another problem by themselves.

After the teacher demonstrates how to find the common denominator to figure out which fraction is larger, she explains how to compare the quantities by converting the fractions into decimals.

Teacher: What is a fast way to convert fractions into decimals?

Student: Mentally? Like, ¾ is point 75.

Teacher: What about $\frac{6}{7}$? You need a calculator to figure that out.

ANALYSIS: The teacher answers her own question of which method she considers more efficient. However, it is unclear if students really learned how to compare fractions using a common denominator or by converting to decimals.

CONCLUSIONS: Effective discussions require students to be cognitively engaged in sense-making, to use their prior knowledge, to ask meaningful questions that build on each other, and to draw or make representations that support their thinking. The big idea the teacher wants the students to grasp during this discussion is what it means to divide and the relationship between decimals and fractions. If we examine the transcript closely, we find that students are not engaged in problem solving. Students are either guessing at the correct answer or performing calculations to answer the question. There is very little opportunity for students to make connections between ideas. Students are willing to participate, but classroom routines that support discussion and sense-making seem to be nonexistent.

REFLECTION QUESTIONS

1. What suggestions would you give this teacher to get these students to talk?

2. What kinds of questions would you have posed if you were the teacher?

3. What mathematical goals and objectives would you have set for this lesson?

Case Study 2: Examining a Successful Discussion

The teacher in Case Study 1 took part in a professional development course and worked on improving her discussion techniques. She applied some of the strategies presented in this book and specifically worked on changing her classroom routines for discussion. Case Study 2 takes place a year later. This time, she approaches teaching comparing fraction quantities differently. She starts the lesson by posing a problem for students to solve. Students work individually, and then share with partners. After students have had a chance to think about this problem, she begins her whole class discussion. Bonnie shares her solution.

> *Bonnie:* ¾ is bigger than ⅔.
>
> *Teacher:* Can you explain to me why you think ¾ is bigger than ⅔?
>
> *Bonnie:* Because four is larger than three.

ANALYSIS: The teacher asks students to justify their reasoning for their answers. Even though the student arrived at the correct answer, her reasoning showed that she had a misconception that needed to be addressed.

> *Teacher:* Does anyone agree with Bonnie?
>
> *Drew:* I think ¾ is bigger than ⅔ because I drew a picture.
>
> *Teacher:* Can you draw the picture on the board?

ANALYSIS: Asking the class if they agree with Bonnie's explanation brings other students into the discussion; they are expected to listen and think about another student's solution. Drew's picture of two circles divided into thirds and fourths allows the class to visualize the problem and solution.

The teacher focuses the class back on the initial misconception; Bonnie's solution ignored the numerator when comparing the fraction quantity. She asks the class if they can rely on only looking at the denominators to make a decision about which fraction is larger. Students conclude that they cannot rely on the denominators alone to tell them which quantity is bigger. When they look at the model they observe that one third is actually bigger than one fourth. However, when they took into account the numerators, the ¾ was actually bigger.

Teacher: So, what else would you do? What is something you were taught to do to compare fractions? Nicole?

Nicole: Find a common denominator.

The student explains how to find the common denominator. Students at this point make a connection between the common denominator and the visual model. Another student raises his hand and comments that he used percent to figure out his answer. He shares his strategy for comparing fractions.

CONCLUSION: As you can see, the routines for discussion have changed. Students now provide justification and representations for their answers and make sense of each other's answers. The teacher activates student's prior knowledge during the lesson, giving them time to think about the problem ahead of time. Students are able to agree and disagree respectfully. The level of engagement and participation reveals that students understand the math concept, contribute to the discussion, and develop their thinking.

REFLECTION QUESTIONS

1. What kind of routines would you like to establish in your class for students to make their thinking explicit to the group?

2. What is the role of the teacher in helping students make their thinking explicit?

3. How does writing down explanations for the whole group help the discussion?

Chapter Summary

Effective whole class discussions require a classroom environment that is nonthreatening and allows students to feel comfortable and confident about sharing and critiquing ideas. A positive classroom community needs to be cultivated. Specifically, students need to feel connected to the teacher and each other, and need to treat each other with respect. Physical classroom routines are necessary to prepare for class discussions and social routines facilitate communication and active listening during the discussion. Routines for communication allow students time to use what they already know, independently think about the problem, share ideas with peers, and then discuss ideas as a class.

Many teachers report that their students are not used to communicating their thinking. Furthermore, teachers are concerned about finding time to have discussions. However, as these teachers worked on having whole group discussions, they found that their students opened up and were more willing to share ideas. Teachers also commented that students retained what they learned in class discussions, which meant they needed less review time during subsequent lessons and could easily build off previous concepts covered in class discussions. Discussions contributed to student learning of mathematics and, most importantly, these teachers found that students became excited about doing math.

STUDY GUIDE

Below is a suggested sequence of activities designed to help you think about the kinds of physical and social classroom routines needed to facilitate effective whole class discussions. Remember, these routines do not develop immediately. They take time to implement and refine.

Evaluate Physical and Social Classroom Routines

1. Watch Video Clips 3.1–3.4. Think about how physical and social classroom routines contribute to discussions in both classrooms.

2. Read the *Video Case Study* on the next page.

3. As you watch the video clips from this chapter and read the *Video Case Study*, use the *Reflecting on Video Clips* worksheet to refine your ability to observe and notice classroom routines. How do they contribute to discussions?

   Note: The ability to notice what is going on in the classroom requires paying attention to details. The questions in the *Reflecting on Video Clips* worksheet will help you practice paying attention to details, which you can then apply to your own classroom.

Try It Out!

Practicing Teacher

1. Once you have thought about how physical and social classroom routines affect class discussions, try some of the ideas listed in *Strategies for Your Classroom*. Remember, don't try all these strategies out at once! Pick a few and work on them.

2. Complete the *Reflecting on Practice* worksheet.

3. Continue adding and removing strategies as appropriate for your classroom.

Pre-Service Teacher

4. Think about the strategies and ideas from the videos and *Strategies for Your Classroom* and try them out as you student teach or in a practicum setting.

5. Complete the *Reflecting on Practice* worksheet.

Reflect and Refine

1. As you continue trying out various strategies, use the *Reflecting on Your Practice* worksheet to think about and adjust what you are doing. Using these tools and the provided rubrics will give you opportunities to

monitor your performance and self-correct as needed. For these types of routines to become automatic, you must have consistent expectations and practice routines daily.

2. Ask yourself if you have built a supportive classroom learning community where students feel comfortable to share their ideas and take risks. What can you do to make the environment more supportive? Is there anything you need to modify?

Tool Box: PDToolkit

- Video Clips 3.1, 3.2, & 3.3
- *Video Case Study:* Second Grade Measurement Lesson and Teacher Interview
- *Strategies for Your Classroom:* Ideas for Developing Classroom Routines
- *Reflecting on Video Clips*
- *Reflecting on Practice:* Building a Supportive Classroom Community
- *Reflecting on Practice:* Thinking about Physical and Social Routines for Discussion
- *Reflecting on Practice:* Routines for Listening
- *Student Self-Evaluation Checklist for Participation in Whole Class Discussion*
- *Whole Class Student Participation Checklist*
- PowerPoint: Chapter 3—Cultivating Classroom Routines for Student Participation

VIDEO CASE STUDY

Second Grade Measurement Lesson and Teacher Interview

Class: Grade 2 / **Teacher:** Ms. Rivara

The Lesson

Ms. Kelsey Rivara teaches second grade in a parochial school in Reno, Nevada and this is her first year teaching. She teaches a class of approximately thirty students. Video Clip 3.3, Second Grade Measurement Lesson, shows Ms. Rivara teaching a lesson on measurement. Her goal for the lesson is to teach students the concept of having a standard unit of measurement (a foot) by using a nonstandard unit of measurement (cutouts of students' shoes). Ms. Rivara hopes that by demonstrating an ineffective method of measurement, students will understand the concept behind a more efficient method of measurement. Ms. Rivara's lesson includes representations, individual work, small group discussions, and whole class discussion. She explains how she uses discussions to support student learning by letting them discuss and learn from each other:

> Whole class discussion is very beneficial because you are given the opportunity to hear what kids have to say. When students hear other students talk, it allows them to better understand the idea of the concept. . . .
>
> If students have misconceptions, then other students can answer [and it might be in] language that [the other students] can understand. Another thing is thinking about thinking. If a student does not understand the one way I am saying it, . . . another student might be able to say it in a way another student can understand it.

PD TOOLKIT™
for *Whole Class Mathematics Discussions*
View the video online at PDToolkit.

Setting Up Physical Routines

Watch the first seven minutes of Video Clip 3.3 and observe how Ms. Rivara uses physical routines to set up the discussion. Reflect on the following questions:

1. How does Ms. Rivara communicate behavioral expectations?

2. What signals does Ms. Rivara use to get student attention?

3. What routines are in place for students to get the materials and supplies needed to participate in the activity?

4. Is there opportunity for each student to actively participate and engage in thinking prior to discussion?

Video Clip 3.4 Second Grade Teacher Interview: Teaching Measurement (00:01:36)

Using Representations to Conduct Discussion

Watch the remainder of the video. Observe how representations are incorported into the lesson. Consider these questions:

1. How does the chart in which Ms. Rivera records students' measurements aid their comprehension?

2. How do students record their thinking and use representations?

3. Observe opportunities for small-group discussion and whole class discussion. What effect do they have on student comprehension?

Conclusions

Physical Routines: Getting Ready for the Discussion

A signal is used to get students' attention for discussion. Ms. Rivara rings a bell and counts to five to alert students to listen for further directions. Next, she provides each student a piece of construction paper and asks students to trace and cut out the shape of their shoe. Students work at their tables to cut the shoe pattern. As students complete the task, Ms. Rivara directs students to sit at their tables and get ready for the whole class discussion. She counts: "Five, four, three, two, one," and gives specific directions. "You show me that you are done if you are sitting in your seats and your yellow paper is in the middle of your table." Younger students need these clear and specific directions to understand expected behaviors. The simplicity and clarity makes it possible for students to follow the directions.

Using Representations to Conduct Discussion

As students use their representations to independently measure the table, they record their thinking and ask each other for help as needed. Ms. Rivara gives specific directions for each student to measure the length and width of the table. As a result, each child is given the opportunity to experience measuring and think about how to use the construction paper foot as the unit of measure.

Students are given a higher-level question to think about as they measure the table. "Did everyone get the same measurement of the table? Why or why not?" Students not only examine their own measurements but also think about why their peers recorded different measurements.

Communicating During Whole Class Discussions

Students use discussion to build on each other's answers. They refer to the chart in which Ms. Rivara recorded the measurments. The chart enables students to see and analyze the range of answers. The class concludes that different size shoes yield different answers. Students further explore how a longer shoe and a smaller shoe can produce different answers. After students conclude why the nonstandard unit produced different answers, the teacher asks students to think about the term *foot*. They discuss what they understand about a foot in small groups, then come together as a class to share their findings. During this time, they explore the standard unit of measure (a foot) by measuring the tables with a ruler and finding out if they reach the same answer. They also discuss the value of using a standard unit of measure.

Ideas for Developing Classroom Routines

Routines for Preparing for Discussions

To prepare for discussions, students should:

- Think about the problem independently.
- Draw pictures, use manipulatives, or write down the steps used to help solve the problem. Students need to be prepared to explain their reasoning.
- Think hard about the problem they are trying to solve.
- Expect to share ideas with others.
- Keep records of thinking in the form of a journal or notebook.

Routines for Communicating Thinking So That Others Can Understand

To work on communicating so their peers can understand what they are saying, students should:

- Use visuals/drawings and models to explain their thinking.
- Explain what the visuals/drawing means.
- Share and develop ideas with a partner or in a small group.
- Ask other students if they understand his or her thinking.
- Ask another student to help clarify thinking.

Routines for Active Listening and Making New Connections

To practice active listening and making new connections, students should:

- Look at and listen to someone who is giving an explanation.
- Ask questions if they don't understand what someone is saying.
- Tell how his or her explanation is similar to or different from other explanations.
- Think about what they are learning about the mathematical concept being discussed.
- Respond to ideas constructively and politely.

Proving or Defending a Position

Use these models and sentence frames to discuss ideas.

- Can you prove your answer?
- I agree with (name) or I disagree with (name).
- My reasoning is similar to /different from yours because . . .
- I think I heard you say . . . Did I say what you meant?
- I'm stuck. Can someone help me?
- This chart shows what I mean.
- This part of my solution is similar to . . . but . . .

REFLECTING ON VIDEO CLIPS

Video Clip 3.1: Student Interview: Cultivating a Classroom Community

1. What are students' perspectives' on classroom community and math talk?
2. Why do they believe it is important for a teacher to have good rapport with them? How does this contribute to a classroom community?
3. What insights did you gain as a result of watching this video clip?

Video Clip 3.2: Fifth & Sixth Grade Teacher Interview: Using Flexible Grouping

1. Why do teachers use flexible grouping?
2. What do they do to facilitate active thinking and discussion?
3. What did this video make you think about?

Video Clip 3.3: Second Grade Measurement Lesson and Teacher Interview

Watch the first seven minutes of the video, observing how Ms. Rivara uses physical routines to set up the discussion. Then consider the following questions.

1. How does Ms. Rivara communicate behavioral expectations?
2. What signals does Ms. Rivara use to get student attention?
3. What routines are in place for students to get the materials and supplies needed to participate in the activity?
4. Is there opportunity for every child to actively participate and engage in thinking prior to discussion?

Watch the remainder of the video. Observe how representations are incorporated into the lesson.

1. How does the chart in which Ms. Rivera records students' measurements aid their comprehension?
2. How do students record their thinking and use representations?
3. Observe opportunities for small-group discussion and whole class discussion. What effect do they have on student comprehension?

Reflect on Video Clip 3.3 as a whole and consider the following questions:

1. What is the teacher's perspective on whole class discussions?
2. What are the implications for teaching math?
3. What did you think about as you watched the interview?

REFLECTING ON PRACTICE

Building a Supportive Classroom Community

1. Do students feel comfortable in the classroom? What can you do to establish mutual respect?

   _____

   _____

   _____

2. How often do you assign students to work with different partners or small groups so that students get the opportunity to know each other?

   _____

   _____

   _____

3. Describe a lesson in which students shared personal experiences and informally used their home language as they developed their understanding of math concepts. What was successful about this lesson? How can you build future lesson plans on this success?

   _____

   _____

   _____

4. What are the strengths and weaknesses of your classroom routines?

   _____

   _____

   _____

5. What changes would you like to make? Why? How will you teach these routines?

   _____

   _____

   _____

REFLECTING ON PRACTICE

Thinking about Physical and Social Routines for Discussion

As you create a math lesson, address the following considerations.

1. What is the math objective of your lesson?

_____

_____

_____

2. What physical routines are needed for this lesson? Describe materials needed, the signal used to begin the physical routine, and the purpose-setting question.

_____

_____

_____

_____

_____

_____

3. Describe how the math objectives can be supported through discussions.

Individual work:

_____

_____

_____

Small-Group Discussion:

_____

_____

_____

Whole Class Discussion:

_____

_____

_____

Continues on next page

Reflecting on Practice, continued

4. Identify how students communicate math in your classroom or a classroom that you are observing. What social routines do students use to participate in the discussion? Evaluate their effectiveness. Can social routines for communication be improved so that for all students can participate in discussion and learn the mathematics concepts?

_____

_____

_____

5. Anticipate what kinds of representations may be created during the lesson. Think about how these various kinds of representations can be used for sense-making during the discussion.

_____

_____

_____

6. What are the strengths and weaknesses of how students communicate their ideas in your classroom? Are other students able to understand the explanations? Are routines in place to aid students' communication?

_____

_____

_____

Routines for Listening

1. What do your students do to listen to the class conversation? Are they engaged in the conversation? Are they able to follow other students' explanations and think about their own explanations? Is there a purpose for students to listen?

   _____

   _____

2. What are the strengths and weaknesses in your current classroom routines?

   _____

   _____

3. What would you modify? Why?

   _____

   _____

4. Describe the kinds of communication that take place during a classroom discussion.

   _____

   _____

   • Is it a group conversation in which the whole class is engaged in discussion?

   _____

   _____

   • Is the conversation between only the teacher and student?

   _____

   _____

   • Are all students participating in the discussion or only a few students participating?

   _____

   _____

Student Self-Evaluation Checklist for Participation in Whole Class Discussion

This checklist is intended for student use. Students will either check the box or fill in an explanation in the rubric to monitor and self-assess their participation in discussions over time. Keeping track of participation will make expectations for participation in discussion explicit. This rubric addresses preparing for discussion using representations, communicating ideas, listening and asking questions, and analyzing other students' ideas.

Name: _____

Date	I prepared for the discussion by thinking about the problem, solving the problem, and drawing/writing down my ideas.	I communicated my ideas clearly by using representations when needed.	I listened to the discussion and asked questions when confused.	I analyzed other students' ideas.

Whole Class Student Participation Checklist

This checklist is intended for instructor use. Create a class list to record how students participate in discussions. Teachers can specifically monitor how students prepare for discussion, communicate their ideas, listen to each other, and analyze ideas presented. This list can help identify strengths and weaknesses of classroom routines for discussion.

Date: _____ Title: _____

Student name	Preparing for discussion (solve problem, show work, and be ready to share thinking)	Presenting ideas so that others can understand representation	Listening (includes asking questions if confused)	Analyzing ideas presented

What Do We Talk About?
Planning the Discussion

We understand something if we see how it is related or connected to other things we know.

(Hiebert, 2003)

A well-planned whole class discussion efficiently uses class time to support the learning of *all* students. Learning happens when students make connections between what they already know and new information (National Research Council, 2001). This means the conversation must build on students' prior knowledge and conceptions. When planning the discussion, teachers need to think about what students know, errors or misconceptions they may have, types of strategies they are using, and the mathematical goals of the lesson. In addition, the whole class discussion must be situated within the long-term and short-term goals. Chapter one introduced three levels associated with planning discussions for one topic (Table 1.2). In this chapter, we cover how to build a year-long curriculum around whole class discussions. To help you build your curriculum, there are three levels of planning: (1) identifying long-term and short-term goals and figuring out how they connect, (2) planning the actual lesson prior to teaching the lesson, and (3) planning during the lesson based on student reasoning and sense-making.

Planning the Lesson to Optimize Learning

Figure 4.1 illustrates the process and considerations to address when planning a lesson. The first step is to identify the mathematical goals of the lesson, where that goal fits into the year-long curriculum, and the possible methods of reasoning students will use. These higher-level views will guide you to identify the "big mathematical ideas" and the skills students should learn to support the big ideas. When teachers are clear about mathematical goals throughout each lesson, it becomes much easier to facilitate mathematical discussion that supports learning math. Student reasoning, misconceptions, and errors serve as starting points for the discussion.

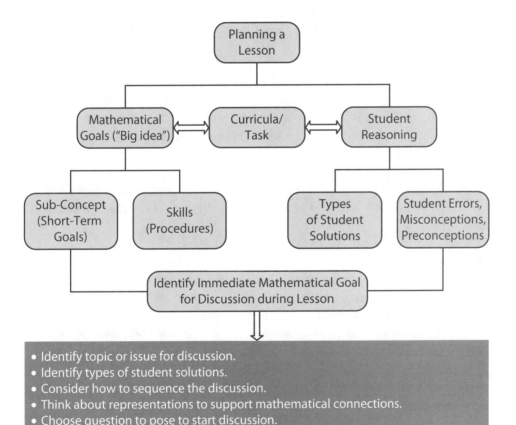

FIGURE 4.1
The whole class discussion planning process

70

What Do We
Talk About?
Planning the
Discussion

Mathematical Goals, Concepts, and Skills

The Common Core standards identify the concepts students should understand and the skills they should develop at each grade level. The Common Core standards list the "big mathematical ideas" and break them down into smaller sub-concepts. An overarching grade 4 standard is "Use place value understanding and properties of operations to perform multi-digit arithmetic." This goal is broken down into the following standards:

4. NBT.4. Fluently add and subtract multi-digit whole numbers using the standard algorithm.

4. NBT.5. Multiply a whole number of up to four digits by a one-digit whole number, and multiply two two-digit numbers, using strategies based on place value and the properties of operations. Illustrate and explain the calculation by using equations, rectangular arrays, and/or area models.

The "big idea" that students need to understand is the concept of place value and properties of operations. The sub-concept covers properties of addition (e.g., if zero is added to a number, the number will remain the same; if two whole numbers are added, the quantity increases). Students show understanding of place value concepts and properties of addition when they explain how they used methods and representations to add multi-digit numbers. The skill that students should become proficient at is the ability to fluently add and subtract multi-digit numbers using a standard algorithm.

State standards, the NCTM Principles and Standards, and curriculum and pacing guides also identify concepts and skills that students should learn. (See the references for books that contain research on mathematical concepts ranging from grades 1–8.)

A mathematical discussion must be thought of as a conversation that takes place over time. Learning happens when students make mathematical connections *within* and *across* lessons. Therefore, it is essential to identify the connections between the larger mathematical concepts, which are long-term goals, and the immediate short-term mathematical goals of the lesson. Each lesson must be situated within a larger context. By prioritizing what is important and planning ahead, instructional time can be used more efficiently and effectively. In addition, students are more likely to learn concepts more quickly when they can see these connections.

What Does It Mean to Understand a Concept or "Big Idea"?

Developing proficiency in mathematics includes developing *conceptual understanding* of mathematical concepts (Star, 2005). Understanding a math concept involves assimilating several layers of inter-connected meaning. For example, consider the part–whole concept of ½ as illustrated in Figure 4.2. Just because a student memorizes that the written symbol ½ can be read as "one half" does not mean the student really understands the concept of ½. It can represent a quantity; ½ of a pie can represent a part–whole relationship.

Some students may view ½ as one piece of the pie, and visualize it as a single unit. However, students can only make the connection that ½ represents a fraction when they make the connection that it is part of the whole unit— the 1 represents the numerator and the 2 represents the denominator. The numerator represents one piece of the pie that has been cut into two equal pieces. The ½ can also be viewed as a division relationship, where the one whole is being equally divided between two people. In this situation, the ½ represents a fair sharing situation where students must also understand the concept of equivalency (equal size pieces). This requires understanding where to physically cut (partition) the pie, so that it yields two equal size pieces.

Students not only need to understand mathematical concepts, they also need to understand *how* to use procedures to appropriately solve problems. When students understand *why* a procedure works, they are also more likely to remember and use the procedure properly in a variety of situations. For example, to identify a fraction, we cut the whole into the specified number that is represented in the denominator. Then we identify the specified number of parts given in the problem. Understanding the concept of half is more than just being able to write the number symbol and say out loud the word *half*. Helping students develop proficiency in math involves helping them develop a rich understanding of mathematics so that they see mathematical connections. For example, visualize ½ using different units. What is ½ of a box of cookies? What is ½ of an hour? What is ½ of a case of soda?

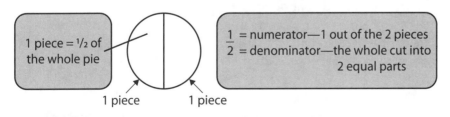

FIGURE 4.2

Conceptually understanding ½ as part of a whole

72

What Do We
Talk About?
Planning the
Discussion

Using a Concept Map to Show Connections

A concept map (Novak & Cañas, 2008) is a useful graphic tool for identifying key relationships and connections between mathematical concepts and ideas. In a concept map, information is organized in connected boxes or circles to indicate hierarchical relationships of ideas. The "big ideas" are the guiding principles of what students should learn; the sub-concepts are usually the short-term goals in lessons that lead up to the development of the larger goals and concepts. A concept map is useful because learning is not necessarily linear. If topics come up during the discussion that fit the bigger picture, the teacher can help students make connections. Concept maps identify potential topics for discussion and serve as road maps to prioritize topics and make decisions on how to support student learning based on mathematical goals. However, a concept map is only a guide; what actually happens during teaching is dictated by what the students do and say. In other words, the plans must be flexible and open to change based on what actually happens in class. Figure 4.3 is a concept map for division that results in a fractional answer.

Quotient is a division relationship that can be written as a/b or $a \div b$, and that results in an answer that has a fraction. For example, consider the problem: "If 3 children equally share one chocolate bar, how much chocolate will each child get?" The division relationship can be written as $1/3$ or $1 \div 3$. Each child will get one third ($1/3$) of a chocolate bar. The one-third chocolate bar represents part of the whole candy bar. Understanding the whole number division relationship that results in a fractional answer ($a \div b = a/b$) involves understanding the meaning of division, the part–whole concept of a fraction, and the expression of the division relationship as a number sentence ($a \div b$ or a/b). Other related ideas that are important for understanding fractions as quotients are the concepts of equivalence, unit, and partitioning.

Equivalency involves understanding the meaning of "equal shares" of the unit. Understanding of equivalency is necessary for understanding a fraction as a quotient. Dividing a whole unit into parts requires understanding of what makes an "equal part" or an equal share. The whole unit the children are sharing is the candy bar. Look at the diagrams in Figure 4.4. Which diagram represents a candy bar divided into three equal parts?

Even though Figure 4.4a is cut into three parts, the parts are not equal; none of the parts will represent a third. Figure 4.4b represents equal parts. Knowing how to cut or partition is important to be able to successfully solve the problem.

As the discussion above demonstrates, helping students develop conceptual understanding of fractions as quotients is not a linear process. It is much easier for students to understand ($a \div b = a/b$) concept if they can connect the underlying mathematics to real world contexts. Table 4.1 illustrates

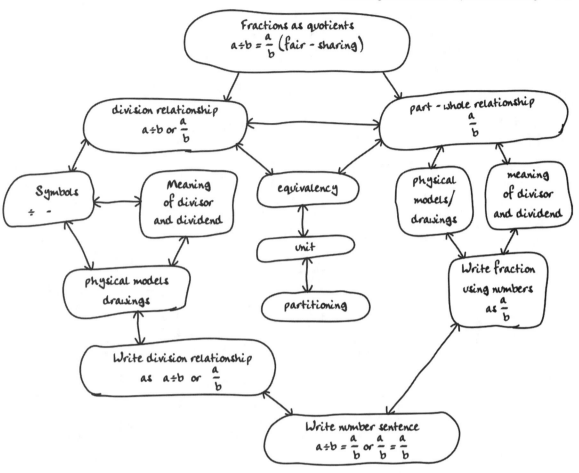

FIGURE 4.3
Concept map for quotients as fractions

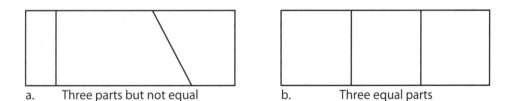

a.   Three parts but not equal   b.   Three equal parts

FIGURE 4.4
What does equal mean?

TABLE 4.1   Fifth-Grade Lesson on Quotients: Phases of Classroom Instruction

Phase	Focus of Classroom Activity	Forms of Reasoning	Key Transitional Strategies
I Representing Quotient as the Answer to a Fair Sharing Problem	Partitioning: Transforming a whole into countable units. Understanding equivalency of shares. How many pieces make up a share? Representing answer as a fraction. Conceptualizing magnitude of fractional answer.	Primarily Pictorial: Partitioning and assigning.	Directing students' attention to the magnitude of the partitions, and the composition of shares—away from "how many?" to "how much?" Presentation of problem contexts that could be represented by a "mixed number"—a quotient with a whole number portion and a fractional portion.
II Symbolizing Fair Sharing Problem Using Standard Divisor and Dividend Notation	Determining the meanings ascribed to the divisor and dividend in $a \div b$ notation. Mapping the meanings of partitions and whole from Phase I onto $a \div b$. Symbolically representing fair sharing as division, with a fractional answer.	"Stuff to split" became defined as the dividend (unit). The number of groups receiving equal shares became defined as the divisor (partitions). The bar in the fractional notation came to represent division; "You divide the stuff to split by the number of groups."	Confront conception that "bigger number must divided by smaller" through examination of problem context. Consistently pairing $a \div b$ notation with the introduction of number sentences: $$a \div b = \frac{a}{b}$$ Using multiplicative relationship as a conceptual support: $$a \times b = c \qquad c \div b = a$$ where a, b, or c could be <1.
III Flexible Use of Fraction and Division Notation with Conceptual Understanding	Examining the relative magnitude of divisor and dividend to anticipate quotient. Predicting the answer to a fair sharing problem without computation: $$6 \div 9 = \frac{6}{9}$$ and $$6 \div 9 < 1$$ Switch to symbolizing division relationship first, then computing and symbolizing answer. Proving correctness of answers by using inverse operation	Anticipating the magnitude of the result of fair sharing as being either greater than or less than 1. Developing a rule for determining if quotient is greater than or less than one. Connecting the previously separate symbolizations for division and fractions **conceptually**—e.g., recognizing that they are the same. Prior to this phase, students focused on figuring out how to symbolize the division relationship and fractional answer separately.	Now pictorial representations justify reasoning following an attempt at solving fair sharing problems, as opposed to being used as tools to come up with solutions.

Reprinted by Permission of SAGE Publications. Lamberg, T. D., & Middleton, J.A., *Educational Researcher* 4(38), pp. 240, 2009.

the phases of instruction that took place in a fifth-grade teaching experiment (Lamberg & Middleton, 2010) that supported students in learning about the quotient interpretation of fraction ($a \div b = a/b$).

Curriculum Tasks and Sequencing

Planning math lessons and thinking about sequencing a discussion is easier when teachers anticipate the path their students might follow to learn the concept. Lessons should be planned as a logical progression of the development of mathematical concepts. Table 4.1 represents the order in which students developed their understanding of fractions as quotients. Math curriculum is usually sequenced; lessons are organized so that concepts build on each other. High-quality mathematics curricula follow a problem-solving approach that lends itself to class discussions and contains problems that require higher levels of thinking.

Understanding how the unit within the curricula is organized and how the concepts build on each other is helpful. If you modify curricula or supplement your existing curricula, *make sure you pay attention to how lessons are sequenced* so that the mathematical concepts build on each other in a logical progression. Not sequencing curricula or teaching random lessons without thinking about how they connect and build on each other leads to ineffective teaching and discussions. When choosing problems to solve, consider how students might respond to the tasks, and the range of answers and misconceptions than can occur.

Anticipating student responses involves developing considered expectations about how students might mathematically interpret a problem, the array of strategies—both correct and incorrect—they might use to tackle it, and how those strategies and interpretations relate to mathematical concepts, representations, procedures, and practices that the teacher would like his or her students to learn (Lambert, 2001; Schoenfeld, 1998; Yoshida, 1999, cited in Stigler & Hiebert, 1999; Stein et al., 2008).

Sequencing Lessons

Whole class discussions that build on previous discussions help students make mathematical connections. When students make connections within a lesson as well across related lessons, their learning is enhanced. Therefore, in addition to the mathematics, you also need to consider how the tasks are sequenced. For example, the NCTM hosts a website called Illuminations

76

What Do We
Talk About?
Planning the
Discussion

(http://illuminations.nctm.org) which contains hundreds of lessons that are organized around concepts and build on each other. Five lessons on fractions build students' conceptual understanding of fractions. The first lesson focuses on exploring how fractions can be represented as a linear region by using fraction strips. The second lesson involves ordering fractions from least to greatest and greatest to least. Students must understand what a fraction represents in relation to a whole unit before they are able to compare sizes and order them. Whole class discussions, which connect to previous discussions, facilitate students' discovery of these mathematical connections.

Think about what mathematical concepts you want students to learn. What related sub-concepts are necessary for the students to understand the concept of each lesson? What problem should be posed for students to solve? Is this problem adequate to make students think? Does the problem address the mathematical concepts that you are trying to teach?

Anticipating Student Reasoning: The 5E Lesson Plan

A math lesson that supports discussion should engage students in problem solving; activities should be organized and sequenced to build opportunities for discussion and sense-making. A problem-solving lesson begins with a problem(s) for students to solve. The students work on the problem independently and discuss with a partner or in small groups as the teacher walks around assessing student thinking and work. A problem to discuss is identified for the whole class discussion based on student understanding and mathematical goals.

Problem-solving lessons can be modeled after Roger Bybee's (1997) 5E lesson plan. Although Bybee's plan was intended for teaching science, mathematics teachers have found this model useful because the five parts of the lesson focus on problem solving and reasoning. The 5Es can be used to create specific lesson plans. The following describes in detail each component of the lesson plan.

1. Engage: The teacher poses an interesting question or problem that captures students' attention, activates their prior knowledge, and leads students to begin thinking about the concept. The problem should address the mathematics that students will learn in the lesson. An appropriate problem has the right level of cognitive demand (challenge) so that it requires thinking and problem solving (Smith, Bill & Hughes, 2008). Therefore the problem must:

- require students to engage in thinking, not just repeat a procedure
- allow for multiple ways that it can be solved using a variety of representations
- help students deepen their understanding of mathematics
- engage students' interest

A problem that is too easy and requires minimal thinking is not a good choice for discussion. There would be nothing to talk about. Similarly, a problem that is too hard and doesn't offer students an entry point to figure out how to solve it is not a good choice. The Engage phase should take no more than 10 to 15 minutes, and it should specifically introduce the main concept of the lesson.

2. Explore: After a problem has been posed for students to solve, they should have time to individually reflect on it and then discuss their ideas with a partner or small group. When students are working, the teacher should look for evidence of student thinking and understanding, focusing on types of student strategies and reasoning, errors, and misconceptions. In this phase of the lesson, based on an analysis of student thinking, the teacher should be determining what should be discussed with the whole class. The teacher should listen to conversations, observe student work, pose questions to clarify their thinking or guide them to solve the problem, and consider how representations can help. Teachers can use classroom experiences and draw from research as well (Stein, et al., 2008) to prepare for ways students may think about a problem. The final decision on the problem or issue that is discussed as a whole class must be made as the actual lesson unfolds.

3. Explain: After they have explored a problem, students meet to explain their reasoning. Discussion leads students to recognize patterns and concepts and describe them in their own words. Students also begin to see errors and misconceptions that may have that led them to an incorrect solution. Discussion must also be based on the teacher's assessment of student thinking and work. Chapter 5 elaborates on how to use teacher questioning to have students explain and elaborate on their thinking.

4. Elaborate: The next phase challenges students to develop deeper understanding, an extended conceptual framework, and improved skills. What are some deeper connections students can make beyond the problem discussed? How can their thinking be extended? What mathematics can be abstracted?

5. Evaluate: In the final phase of the instructional model, teachers assess students' learning. Students could solve a related problem or record their

78

What Do We
Talk About?
Planning the
Discussion

thinking in their math journals. The evaluation allows the teacher to gauge what students understood and what can be refined.

Informally assessing student reasoning requires careful observation and analysis of what students are doing and thinking. In video case 1.4, in Chapter 1, the teacher identified five different answers and three ways of student thinking, which became the basis of the whole class discussion. As students explained their reasoning using their schematic drawings, the teacher was able to identify and correct errors, and help students see that there was more than one way to arrive at the correct answer. Examples of students' solutions to two problems involving fractions are presented at the end of this chapter. Analyses of the solutions can be used to help you consider the sequence of the discussion and the order in which students should present their solutions so that students can best make mathematical connections.

Chapter Summary

There are three levels of planning involved in facilitating a whole class discussion that supports learning. The first level involves thinking about the long-term and short-term goals to identify what students need to learn over a period of time. The second level is the individual lesson plan that provides more details and specifics on how to teach particular lessons. When a lesson plan is made for an individual lesson, this lesson is situated within the context of the larger mathematical goals. Discussions are much easier to facilitate and more effective if the teacher is clear about what students should learn, and thinks carefully thinking about *sequencing*. Individual lesson planning involves selecting tasks or problems for students to solve and anticipating how students might respond, what they might have difficulty with, and what prior knowledge is needed. The third level of planning takes place during the lessons. The teacher uses informal assessment to determine whether students are making sense of the planned lesson, and adjusts the discussion accordingly. The teacher identifies student solutions, strategies, errors, and misconceptions and prioritizes a topic for discussion that engages students in deeper level thinking. Decisions based on the third level of planning should build on students' thinking and understanding and consider the specific needs of learners.

STUDY GUIDE

The NCTM and Common Core standards emphasize that students need to understand mathematical concepts and develop procedural fluency. As a teacher, this means you need to think about how to plan and make decisions to facilitate whole class discussions. Setting up your planning according to the three levels will help you think about a discussion as being situated within larger mathematical goals over time. Your goal is to help students make mathematical connections within single lessons, the discussion, and other lessons.

Below is a suggested sequence of activities designed to help you engage in planning and facilitating discussion. These activities should take you a couple of days to work on. This is not something you need to do in one day. Taking the time you need to plan makes your teaching more efficient and effective.

Level 1: Identify Long-Term Goals, Short-Term Goals, and Interconnections

Examine Planning

Reflect on *Strategies for Your Classroom: Three Levels of Planning—Level 2.* Think about how a whole class discussion is situated in larger mathematical goals so that students can make connections.

Long-Term Plan

Gather your district standards, the NCTM or the Common Core standards that you are required to use and identify the "big mathematical ideas" that you need students to understand. It is always helpful to understand year-long goals. This makes creating unit plans more straightforward.

Identify and Research Math Concepts

Once you have identified the big ideas that meet your school's standards, do some research regarding that concept to locate literature discussing the best approaches for conceptual understanding of that topic. You can either look up articles on a particular topic or use a resource such as a math methods textbook, which will summarize the research for you. The research will give you a better understanding of the reasoning behind the standards, possible student reasoning strategies, how to teach these topics, and the kinds of errors and misconceptions students might make.

80

What Do We
Talk About?
Planning the
Discussion

Unit Plan

Create a *concept map* or some graphical organizer that allows you to see how your math concepts connect to other. Identifying what procedures and concepts that students should understand will help you figure out what you need to assess. Use this list to develop an assessment checklist to use while teaching. For example, to teach two-digit addition, students need to understand place value. Add "place value" to your checklist for the lesson so you can be sure that students grasp that concept before moving into two-digit addition. Once you have identified these big ideas and approaches, you can add to your notes over time and refer back to this when you teach the concept the next time.

Practicing Teacher: Have your year-long goals at hand and use this long-term view to focus on developing a concept map one unit at a time. By using your year-long goals, you know what content students need to know and can plan your time accordingly. Use the *Rubric for Unit Planning: Level 1* to sequence how you will teach key ideas. This list gives you a concrete view of standards you are meeting and the time tasks will likely take. This unit plan helps you anticipate what students might do and allows you to quickly see the big picture.

Pre-service Teacher: Focus on one unit at a time. Use one particular concept to plan the full unit. Fill out one line of the *Rubric for Unit Planning: Level 1* and ask for feedback from peers. Consider how that unit would fit into the series of year-long standards you developed in the Long-Term Planning section. Filling out the whole year is a useful exercise, and a great way to get feedback on your classroom planning.

Sequencing

Fill out *Reflecting on Practice: Level 1 Planning* and get feedback on your overall concept map. Next, examine your curricula and sequence your lessons so that they build on each other and fit with your concept map. Don't lay out highly detailed lesson plans, but consider the overall structure of lessons so you can determine if they build appropriately off each other. At this stage, a highly detailed lesson plan will minimize your ability to adapt based on your students' learning abilities as you move through the unit. Your goal is not to create original lesson plans, but to use, refine, and adapt existing high-quality curricula to support your students as they learn math.

Level 2: Plan the Individual Lesson

Examine Planning

Reflect on *Strategies for Your Classroom: Three Levels of Planning—Level 2*. Think about structuring a lesson to meet long-term goals and what kinds of questions you might pose to students to encourage discussion.

Develop the Lesson Plan

Now that you have developed a concept map, identified and sequenced lessons, you are ready to start planning the individual lesson. Use the *Rubric for 5E Lesson Plan: Level 2* to outline your lesson. You don't have to use the provided plan, but if you choose not to, remember to focus on the structure of the lesson. It should lend itself to higher level reasoning, problem solving, and communication. Make sure each section of the lesson plan builds towards the next section. For example, the engagement activity must be linked to the explore activity to develop a concept. To effectively build, you must pay attention to how you sequence a lesson's activities in order to maximize opportunities for students to make mathematical connections. When you teach the lesson, you may find that you have to modify and adapt your plans depending on how students are making sense of the lesson, which is the third level of planning.

> NOTE: If you are a beginning teacher, it helps to write out a detailed lesson plan. If you are an experienced teacher and this is a new approach to teaching, it may help you to write down your thoughts until you have mastered the new lesson plan structure and format.

Level 3: Examine Student Work to Build Whole Class Discussion

Examine Planning

Before class, familiarize yourself with the *Strategies for Your Classroom: Three Levels of Planning—Level 3*. It may be useful to make a copy of this page for yourself as you become familiar with this lesson structure so you can easily remind yourself of helpful strategies for moving into whole-class discussion. Then read the classroom case study that begins on the next page and practice examining student work to plan discussion.

Evaluate student problem solving approaches

The third level of planning takes place during the lesson. You have already assigned students a problem to solve. Now, as they are working, you should

82

What Do We
Talk About?
Planning the
Discussion

walk around the room and examine what students are doing. Reflect on the third level of *Strategies for Your Classroom: Three Levels of Planning* to brainstorm what your next step will be. Also use any insights you gained in your own classroom or practicum setting.

Choose a Topic or Problem for Discussion

Once you have thoroughly evaluated student work, use the *Rubric for Planning the Discussion: Level 3* to plan your whole-class discussion. Identify where students struggle as they try to solve the problem. Think about those areas in relation to the mathematical concept and "big idea" that you are trying to teach. Your goal is to identify a problem to pose to get the discussion started, and to think about sequencing the discussion to help students make mathematical connections by building on each other's work. Remember, plans must always be flexible in order to build on how students respond.

Tool Box: PDToolkit

- *Classroom Case Study:* Analyzing Student Work to Plan Discussion
- *Strategies for Your Classroom:* Three Levels of Planning
- *Reflecting on Practice:* Level 1 Planning
- Rubric for Unit Planning: Level 1
- Rubric for the 5E Lesson Plan: Level 2
- Rubric for Planning the Discussion: Level 3

CLASSROOM CASE STUDY

Analyzing Student Work to Plan Discussion

Choosing a topic for whole class discussion involves analyzing student work and listening to students' conversations. The following classroom example is provided to help you think about how you might plan a discussion based on students' reasoning.

SCENARIO: Fifth-grade students are investigating the division relationship between the divisor and dividend, exploring the fair sharing context and problem as an algebraic relationship between the divisor and dividend ($a \div b = a/b$). Students are able to predict if the answer would be greater or less than one, but some are still struggling to represent the problem context and solution as a number sentence (e.g., $4 \div 5 = 4/5$).

THE TASK: The teacher presents two problems:

1. If 6 children share 8 pies equally, then how much will each child get?
2. If 8 children share 6 pies equally, then how much will each child get?

Students must write a number sentence first and then use pictures to prove their answers. The goal is to have students use mathematical symbols to represent their thinking. After the teacher poses the problems for her students to solve, she walks around the room observing what the students are doing. Solutions of five students are presented on the following pages. Analyze each solution, and answer the questions that follow each student work sample.

Questions

1. What do you anticipate students might do when faced with these two problems?
2. Would you have chosen different problems? Why?

Student Work Sample A: Richard's Solution

Solve the following problems. Make sure you write the number sentence.
Then solve the problem and check your answer.

3. If 6 children share 8 pies equally, then how much will each child get?

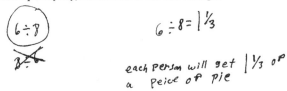

$$6 \div 8 = 1\tfrac{1}{3}$$

each Person will get 1 ⅓ of
a peice of pie

4. If 8 children share 6 pies equally, then how much will each child get?

Hint:
Think about the following:
5. What is the problem asking you to do? It is asking me to give each person
a slice of pie equally.
6. What information is provided in the problem?

#1. 6 children and 8 pies are in this Problem.

#2. 8 children and 6 pies are in this problem.

Reflecting on a Student's Answers

1. What do you think Richard understands?
2. What errors or misconceptions does Richard have?
3. What could be a potential focus of topic for whole class discussion?

ANALYSIS OF RICHARD'S SOLUTION: Richard had difficulty figuring out the order of the divisor and dividend to write the number sentence. He did not solve the first problem. He wrote the division relationship using both numbers. Therefore, it indicates that he was thinking about the order and decided to settle on the incorrect representation. In the second problem, he wrote the reverse division relationship, 8 ÷ 6, and it appears that he made this decision based on his prior answer. He did correctly solve the problem using drawings. Even though he got the correct answer of ¾ and was able to represent each child's share, he did not attempt to write this problem as a division number sentence resulting in ¾ the solution. He was able to correctly identify the numbers in the problem context, the number of children B, and the number of pies to divide. The diffi culty he had was making sense of how to accurately represent the division relationship.

Student Work Sample B: Katie's Solution

Solve the following problems. Make sure you write the number sentence.
Then solve the problem and check your answer.

3. If 6 children share 8 pies equally, then how much will each child get?

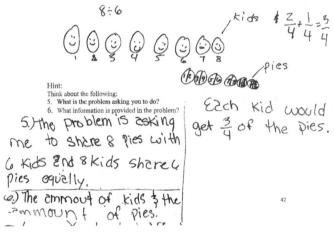

Each person will get 1⅓ of the pies.

4. If 8 children share 6 pies equally, then how much will each child get?

Each kid would get ¾ of the pies.

Hint:
Think about the following:
5. What is the problem asking you to do?
6. What information is provided in the problem?

5.) The problem is asking me to share 8 pies with 6 kids and 8 kids share 6 pies equally.

6.) The ammount of kids & the ammount of pies.

42

Reflecting on a Student's Answers

1. What do you think Richard understands?
2. What errors or misconceptions does Richard have?
3. What could be a potential focus of topic for whole class discussion?

ANALYSIS OF KATIE'S SOLUTION: Katie incorrectly wrote the division relationship in both problems. However, she was able to accurately represent and solve the problem using pictorial representation. Therefore, she understood how to solve the problem even though she was unable to correctly write the number sentence. It is possible she represented the division relationship in the order it was presented in the problem context. Katie had converted the ½ into an equivalent fraction of ½ and she wrote a number sentence of ²⁄₄ + ¼ = ¾. This indicates that she understands equivalent fractions and how to add fractions. Katie did not write a number sentence to represent the division relationship.

Continues on next page

Student Work Sample C: Juan's Solution

Solve the following problems. Make sure you write the number sentence.
Then solve the problem and check your answer.

3. If 6 children share 8 pies equally, then how much will each child get?

4. If 8 children share 6 pies equally, then how much will each child get?

8 childres 6 pies

Hint:
Think about the following:
5. What is the problem asking you to do?
6. What information is provided in the problem?

5. To do a noder sitisin.

6. noder sitisin

Reflecting on a Student's Answers

1. What do you think Juan understands?
2. What errors or misconceptions does Juan have?
3. What could be a potential focus of topic for whole class discussion?

ANALYSIS OF JUAN'S SOLUTION: Juan is able to correctly identify the divisor and dividend in the problem context and set up the problem as a division situation. This is evident because he wrote the key dividend and divisor information explicitly such as "8 children, 6 pies," He understands that the whole unit must be equally partitioned as indicated by his drawing of equal shares. However, he has diffi culty partitioning a unit into equal size pieces and representing the fractional amount symbolically. He has not symbolically represented the division relationship of $a \div b$.

Student Work Sample D: Samantha's Solution

Solve the following problems. Make sure you write the number sentence.
Then solve the problem and check your answer.

3. If 6 children share 8 pies equally, then how much will each child get?

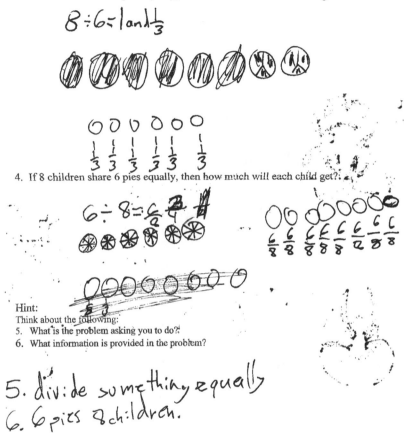

$8 \div 6 = 1 \text{ and } \tfrac{1}{3}$

4. If 8 children share 6 pies equally, then how much will each child get?

$6 \div 8 = \tfrac{6}{8}$

Hint:
Think about the following:
5. What is the problem asking you to do?
6. What information is provided in the problem?

5. divide something equally
6. 6 pies 8 children.

Reflecting on a Student's Answers

1. What do you think Samantha understands?
2. What could be a potential focus of topic for whole class discussion? How can Samantha's thinking/strategy be used in the discussion?

ANALYSIS OF SAMANTHA'S SOLUTION: Samantha solved the problem pictorially first, using smaller circles to represent the children and the larger circles to represent the pies. Then she used the appropriate number sentence to show how to solve the problem. Samantha also understood how to reduce a fraction.

Continues on next page

Student Work Sample E: Conner's Solution

Solve the following problems. Make sure you write the number sentence.
Then solve the problem and check your answer.

3. If 6 children share 8 pies equally, then how much will each child get?

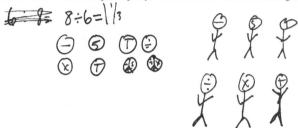

4. If 8 children share 6 pies equally, then how much will each child get?

Hint:
Think about the following:
5. What is the problem asking you to do?
6. What information is provided in the problem?

Reflecting on a Student's Answers

1. What do you think Conner understands?
2. What could be a potential focus of topic for whole class discussion? How can Conner's thinking/strategy be used in the discussion?

ANALYSIS OF CONNER'S SOLUTION: Conner also was able to represent the problem context and solution symbolically as well as justify his answer pictorially. He used a similar strategy to Katie's on the first problem. He distributed the whole pies and then partitioned the two remaining pies into thirds. He used number symbols in his drawings to indicate each person's share. In the second problem he partitioned the pies into fourths and indicated each person's share as representing ¾ of the pie.

An Overall Analysis of Students' Solutions

Reflecting on All Students' Answers

1. What do you think the students understand based on the student solutions you just analyzed?
2. What could be a potential focus of topic for whole class discussion? Why?

What Students Understood

- Most students understood how to accurately represent the division situation using pictorial representations.
- Many students knew how to figure out the answer by partitioning the dividend into equal sized pieces.
- Students used symbols to represent the divisor and dividend and also to represent corresponding share.

What Students Had Difficulty With

- A large majority of the students had difficulty representing the number sentence correctly to represent the division relationship. They understood how to solve problem, but had difficulty remembering the order to represent the divisor and dividend.
- Students did not connect the division sentence with the meaning of dividend and divisor.
- Students did not understand the relationship between the fair sharing context and the solution (algebraic thinking).

Planning the Whole Class Discussion

The teacher has to make a decision about what to discuss in with the whole class. In this case, looking at student reasoning and work, it is clear that students have difficulty writing number sentences to represent problem context and answer. It is possible they were writing the divisor and dividend in the order of how it was presented in the problem context.

In this interview, the teacher explains how she will decide on a topic for discussion.

Interviewer: What are some specific things you do or think about when you are getting your students to understand concepts that they are struggling with?

Teacher: The first place I will look at is misconceptions. . . . One of the things I do a lot is play dumb. I will start out by looking at the wrong answer. I will start out with the common misconceptions they have seen in the past and see what happens. I think that getting at what they already know is key!

Continues on next page

Interviewer: Describe how you assess students' knowledge.

Teacher: Some days I will stand in the middle, or whatever, and watch what is going on. I will usually stop off at the tables and I think to myself, what is it that they have in common? What are they all doing? Usually what I do, is look. Did they do what I wanted them to do?

Interviewer: So how do you use the information? What do you do with it?

Teacher: It tells me where I want to go. It tells me what direction I want to go with it. It tells me what they understand and what they don't. It tells me what they have down and what they don't. . . . And then when I figure out what they are grappling with, then I figure out how to scaffold, how to break it down. I also have a tendency to feel the room, I watch kids. You can see it in their eyes, facial expressions, if they are with you or not with you.

This particular teacher looked at what students were doing; by looking at misconceptions and errors she decided on the direction she wanted to take during whole class discussion. *Strategies for the Classroom: Three Levels of Planning—Level 3* provides suggestions for planning the topics to be discussed with the whole class. This classroom study continues in Chapter 5, which examines teacher questioning in detail.

Reflection Questions

1. What is the value of the teacher walking around and observing student work? What should the teacher pay attention to when examining student work?

2. What is the difference between only looking at student answers to make sure that they are correct versus understanding the process of student thinking in relation to the solution?

3. Examine student work from a lesson you have taught. Identify types of reasoning, errors, and misconceptions. Think about a question you could pose to get a discussion started.

CHAPTER 4 STRATEGIES FOR YOUR CLASSROOM

Three Levels of Planning

Level 1: Identify Long-Term Goals, Short-Term Goals, and Interconnections

- Identify long-term and short-term mathematical goals.
- Identify the concepts students should understand and what procedures they should be able to do.
- Develop a concept map to see how these topics are connected.

Level 2: Plan the Individual Lesson

- Plan the lesson with discussion in mind.
- Select tasks that support the mathematical goals and engage students in reasoning and problem solving.
- Anticipate what students might do and possible topics for discussion.

Level 3: Examine Student Work to Build Whole Class Disscussion

- As students are engaged in solving problems, walk around the room and observe their reasoning processes.
- Record or make mental notes of types of strategies that you see students using. Typically there will be four or five different ways the class is thinking. Consider which strategies are more effective and how the less effective strategies might help you build up to the more effective strategies.
- Pose questions to help students clarify thinking, or provide helpful hints.
- Note misconceptions or errors that should be addressed in the discussion.
- Think about what background knowledge student solutions reveal in order to build discussion on what they already know.
- Think about the "big mathematical idea" you want students to understand as a result of solving the problem.
- Identify a problem or issue to discuss that will challenge students' current thinking and builds on what students are currently doing. Note: Don't try to address every issue that comes up. Prioritize the issues for discussions. Pick one or two important issues to explore in depth.
- Think about sequencing the discussion. In what order should the solutions be presented? The purpose of informally assessing student work and reasoning is to make decisions on how you can support and extend student understanding and thinking. An ineffective use of observation time is checking for correct answers. Checking who has the right and wrong answers will not show you what students understand in terms of conceptual processes. Furthermore, it is inefficient to individually tutor each child and show them "the steps" to solve the problem. When students struggle to solve a problem, they are engaging in sense-making that supports learning.

Level 1 Planning

1. Pick a topic/concept and make your own concept map. Share your concept map with your group to get feedback.

2. What are your long-term and short-term goals?

_____

_____

_____

_____

_____

_____

3. Evaluate the lessons that comprise a unit in your curriculum or textbook. Describe how the mathematical concepts in the lessons build on each other. Share your ideas with your group to get feedback.

_____

_____

_____

_____

_____

_____

Rubric for Unit Planning: Level 1

The purpose of this rubric is to think about sequencing and progression of lessons. Therefore recording the math concepts and skills needed to learn and anticipate how students might respond is helpful in thinking about how to help students make mathematical connections.

Mathematics Topic: _____

Lesson	Math Concept (big ideas) (sub-concepts)	Standard	Skills	Problem to Pose	Anticipated Student Errors, Misconceptions, Preconceptions
1					
2					
3					
4					

Rubric for the 5E Lesson Plan: Level 2

This lesson plan rubric provides a structure for a problem-solving based lesson. This type of structure of a lesson plan lends itself to including discussion as part of the learning process.

Grade: _____ Date: _____ Title of Lesson: _____

Math Topics: _____ Standard(s): _____

Objectives: _____

Materials needed: _____

5Es	Possible Misconceptions	Evidence of Student Reasoning
1. Engage: Questions/Problem to Pose		
2. Explore: Activity/Problem for Independent/Partner/ Small Group		
3. Explain: Whole Class Discussion		
4. Elaborate: Identify "big idea"		
5. Evaluate: Assess learning		

Rubric for Planning the Discussion: Level 3

Use this worksheet during the discussion to informally assess students' thinking, errors, misconceptions, and representations in order to identify an issue to discuss.

Date: _____ Curriculum/Pacing Guide Lesson: _____

Math Concept/Skills	Types of student strategies/errors and misconceptions
Notes on Representations	**Sequencing the discussion (solution types)**
Goals for Discussion	**Problem to pose to get discussion started**

Teacher Questioning and Mathematical Connections

Teachers can effectively use questions during the whole class discussion to help students clarify their thinking and to challenge them to think more deeply about the ideas presented. Chapter 4 discussed how to base a discussion on mathematical goals and how to use observation to understand student reasoning. Students' understanding and conceptions are either refined or changed as they reflect on questions that are posed by the teacher. These questions make a bridge between students' current understanding and your mathematical goals. During a conversation, students typically accept and assimilate each other's ideas, disagree, change their minds, or re-invent new ideas (Martino and Maher, 1999). The next step is learning how to use teacher questioning to facilitate these mathematical connections during the whole class discussion.

> Teacher questioning has been identified as a critical part of teachers' work. The act of asking a good question is cognitively demanding, it requires considerable pedagogical content knowledge and it necessitates that teachers know their learners well.
>
> (Boaler & Brodie, 2004)

Posing a Question to Start the Whole Class Discussion

A question is the best way to begin a discussion. For example, a discussion with young children might begin by asking them if the number sentence $6 + 9 = 7 - 2 + 10$ is true. To answer this question, students will likely use multiple strategies such as $6 + 9 = 5 + 10 = 15$ or $7 - 2 = 5 + 10 = 15$. Some students might conclude that the answer should be 15, because they believe that the answer comes after the equal sign.

This problem can generate a meaningful discussion only if it has the appropriate level of challenge based on student prior knowledge and background. Students should experience some level of difficulty and the problem should potentially result in a range of answers or models. If the problem is too easy, students will know the answer and there will be nothing to talk about. Similarly, choosing a problem that is too difficult for students is not very useful either. Students need to have some entry point for tackling the problem. The mathematical goals for students and their current understanding should guide the direction of the conversation.

Using Questions to Identify Discussion Topics

Guided questions during the discussion can lead students to identify problems and issues to explore and discuss. For example, in one of the problems described in Chapter 4—If 6 children share 8 pies equally, how much pie will each child get?—the teacher might help students figure out how to partition a circle correctly by asking, "How do you decide how many equal parts you need to cut each pie into?" This question requires students to think about the concept of partitioning, equal shares, and fair-sharing situations. Students will have to discover that equal sharing situations require cutting the whole into equal amounts; the whole unit has to be cut into shares that represent multiples of the divisors. In this situation, it is the students, not the teacher, who are defining the problem. As students engage in solving problems individually and in small groups, more questions or issues may come up.

Problem posing can lead to critical thinking and deeper understanding of mathematical ideas (Brown & Walter, 2005). Questions such as "What is the problem really asking?" can be explored. Many times students are unable to solve a problem because they do not understand what the problem is asking them in the first place. "What if" scenarios involve modifying a problem, which requires students to re-conceptualize the problem and use a different approach to problem solve. For example, a student or teacher could ask what would happen if numbers in a problem were changed. For example, what if ten children instead of six shared eight pies equally? What would happen to each child's share? By asking this type of question, the students have to think about the role of the divisor and the dividend in the problem. This can lead to the exploration of the idea that larger the denominator, the smaller the resulting answer. In other words, each child would get less pie because more people are sharing the pies. By modifying the question, students are able to make connections to the "big idea" and understand other applications of the skill they are learning.

After a question has been posed, students need time to work with partners or small groups to think about the problem. The teacher should observe students' reasoning and then choose the order in which students will present their solutions. Students with lower level strategies using more concrete approaches can share first. Students with more abstract and sophisticated strategies can share later. This way, the class can get the opportunity see how ideas build on each other. This allows them to see the progression and interconnections between concrete, abstract, and more efficient strategies. The purpose of the discussion is to engage students in sense-making. The next section describes the different levels of sense-making, and the types of questions that get at these layers of sense-making.

Phase 3: Developing New Mathematical Insights by Making Generalizations (Abstract Mathematical Concepts)

Phase 2: Analyzing Each Other's Solutions to Make Connections (Analyzing Low Level to More Sophisticated Reasoning)

Phase 1: Making Thinking Explicit (Explaining Reasoning)

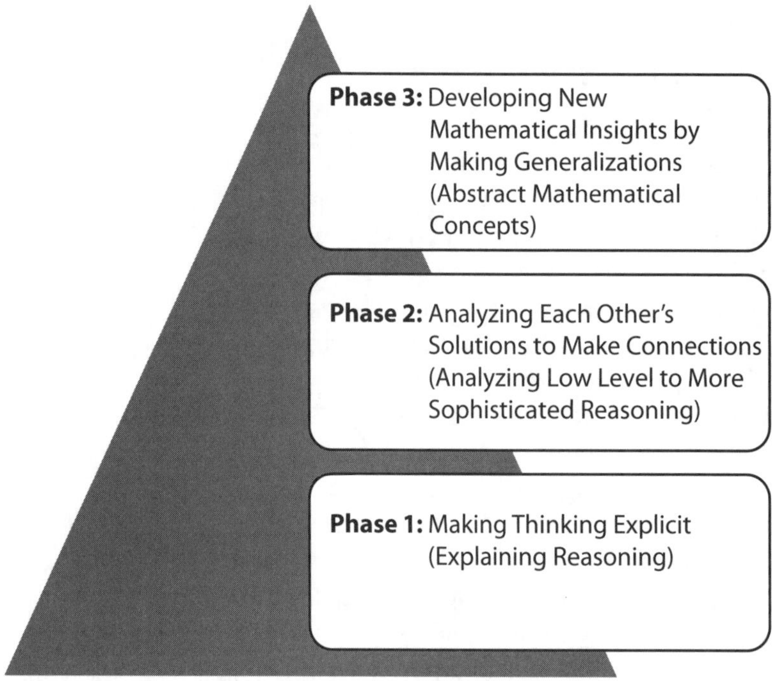

FIGURE **5.1**
Levels of analysis and sense-making in discussions

The Three Levels of Sense-Making in Discussion

Teacher questioning can be used to unpack meaning throughout the three levels of a whole class discussion. Figure 5.1 illustrates the layers of sense-making in a conversation that will lead to new mathematical insights. The first phase involves communicating clearly so that everyone can understand each other's perspective. The second phase involves comparing and analyzing each other's point of view. This is different than just sharing information. A higher level of critical thinking takes place when students evaluate, compare, and contrast each other's strategies and make connections between each other's points of view. The third phase of conversation involves taking the conversation to a much deeper level that leads to mathematical generalizations, or the "big mathematical ideas" at which students arrive. Formal mathematics such as formulas and definitions or a summary of a "big mathematical idea" can be introduced at this point. This is the kind of knowledge that can transfer to other problem situations.

Phase 1: Making Thinking Explicit

Students' explanations make meaningful contributions to the discussion only if the whole class can understand the ideas being presented. An explanation given by a student is useful only when the other students can follow it. Otherwise, students tune out of the conversation or become confused. The teacher can ask questions to scaffold the student's explanation, monitor whether the students understand the explanation and are paying attention, and have students restate the explanation in their own words. Students can use drawings and models to enhance their explanations. Pointing to part of the model or drawing helps the class see what a student is referring to.

The sequence of presentation of the student explanations should be carefully considered. It is much easier to follow student explanations if the ideas are presented from the simpler level to the more sophisticated. This allows students to gain knowledge that will help them understand the more complex ideas. All students do not need to present explanations; it is sufficient to present a few different strategies. Sample questions that can be used to help students explain and clarify their thinking are provided at the end of the chapter.

Case Study 1: Clarifying an Explanation

SCENARIO: The teacher presents this problem to her fifth-grade students: "If 5 children equally shared 6 packs of gum that had 5 pieces in each pack, how much would each child get?" Students can think about the unit in the problem in relation to "packs of gum," "pieces of gum," or simultaneously think in "packs and pieces."

Continues on next page

Case Study, continued

THE DISCUSSION: Sam presents his solution. The teacher poses questions to the class to make sure they understand what Sam is thinking.

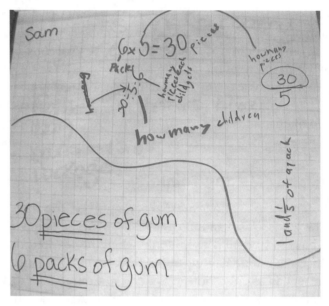

> *Sam*: How many pieces are in a pack? It comes to be 30 pieces of gum. Five sticks represents "how many children." Thirty divided by 5 equals 6, and the 6 equals "how many pieces of gum each child gets."

> *Teacher*: Anyone want to try and explain what he was thinking? Sam did a good job, but sometimes it helps to have another student walk through it. Corey?

FIGURE 5.2
Sam's solution

Corey: I think what Sam was doing was, he was trying to figure out the problem by just using number sentences. Like he is drawing here, it is a really short number sentence. I put these two together to make a true number sentence.

Teacher: Can you tell me how Sam was thinking about the math? You just explained his method. Walk us through what exactly Sam was doing here.

Corey: Well, what I think he was doing was that he was writing the number sentences.

Teacher: Can you explain what each of those pieces represents in the number sentence? I notice that the 6 in the number sentence is not labeled. What do you think the 6 represents?

Corey: I would think that the 6 represents pieces or something.

Karen: It represents the six-pack.

Teacher: It represents the pack? Would you add that word there?

ANALYSIS: Sam provided an explanation; however because the teacher did not feel that the students understood his explanation, she asked another student to explain what Sam was thinking so that students would analyze his solution. Corey pointed out that Sam did not draw a picture like the other students had; instead he used number sentences to represent his work. To make students dig deeper into Sam's mathematical thinking, the teacher re-directed the conversation and asked more specific questions. She asked what the numbers in Sam's number sentence represented in relation to the problem. She wanted students to notice that Sam was thinking about the unit in terms of packs and pieces: 6×5 represented 6 packs of gum times 5 pieces in each pack, for a total of 30 pieces. The teacher wanted students to understand the larger mathematical goal that visualizing the unit can influence how you solve the problem. Furthermore, there are many ways to visualize the unit.

Phase 2: Analyzing Each Other's Solutions to Make Connections

When students are expected to analyze each other's solutions, they need to think about the student's explanation, decide if the answer makes sense, and if the answer connects to other ideas presented in the discussion. The students must be actively listening to benefit from the discussion. (Chapter 3 described what active listening looks like.) When students listen and actively participate, they will eventually learn that listening and thinking about their own explanations supports their own learning (Martino & Maher, 1999). In other words, as they listen, they should think about how what another student is saying relates to their thinking. Therefore, students have to engage in critical thinking instead of passively listening to student explanations. For example, to solve a fair sharing problem, one student might come up with a solution of ½ and another with ¾. Students can deepen their understanding of mathematics by examining how these solutions are similar and different. For example, a student can prove that ¾ and ½ are the same amount. On the other hand students can explore that even though they are equivalent, the whole unit is partitioned differently. In addition, students are also learning that the problem can be solved in multiple ways, which leads to flexibility in thinking and number sense.

Comparing solutions also enables students to see connections between simpler and more sophisticated answers. In addition, students also need to work towards developing more efficient strategies for solving problems (Cobb, Yackel, & McClain, 2000). For example, there are many ways to solve the problem 20 ÷ 5. The following solutions are presented from simple to more sophisticated and represent a continuum from least to most efficient:

1. distribute 20 blocks into 5 piles and count how many pieces are in a pile

2. draw 20 circles and circle groups of 5

3. use tally marks grouped in 5's

4. add 5 + 5 + 5 + 5

5. multiply 5 × 4

Eventually, students should work towards using more efficient strategies to accurately solve problems; however, understanding how the inefficient strategies contribute to the more efficient strategies develops students' number sense. For example, if students don't have an image that 5 × 4 is really 5 groups of 4, then they really don't have a deep understanding of multiplication as a concept. Just memorizing 5 × 4 = 20 without understanding what it means is a shallow understanding of mathematics. If students forget the memorized answer, they may be unable to figure out the answer using another method or use this knowledge as a tool to solve other problems.

The goal is to use discussion to help students develop these layers of understanding, which in turn helps them develop proficiency in mathematics. Figure 5.3 illustrates the continuum of understanding from inefficient to efficient strategies that is listed above. The ultimate goal is for students to become proficient in solving mathematical problems using the most efficient strategies.

Understanding the meaning of symbols and their mathematical meaning has been called "mathematizing" (Cobb, Yackel, & McClain, 2000). Students develop more sophisticated understanding of mathematics through discussion using drawings and models to represent thinking. Because students don't naturally make connections, the teacher can pose questions to help students see how strategies relate to each other. When students see connections between various strategies, they develop more sophisticated understanding of mathematics in addition to number sense. Furthermore, students who have varied ability levels in solving the problem are able to participate in the conversation.

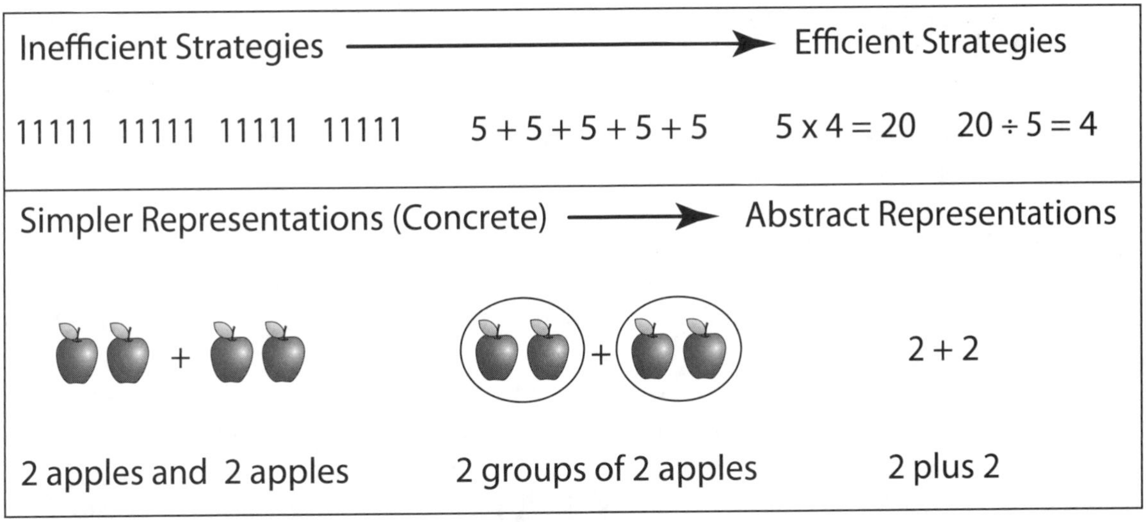

Inefficient Strategies ——————————→ Efficient Strategies

11111 11111 11111 11111 $5 + 5 + 5 + 5 + 5$ $5 \times 4 = 20$ $20 \div 5 = 4$

Simpler Representations (Concrete) ——————→ Abstract Representations

2 apples and 2 apples   2 groups of 2 apples   2 plus 2

FIGURE 5.3

Continuum of levels of understanding and student strategies

Phase 3: Developing New Mathematical Insights by Making Generalizations

The purpose of the discussion is to help students gain new mathematical insights that can transfer to new problem solving situations. After students have explored different strategies to solve a problem, they need to clearly understand the underlying mathematics concepts they learned. Therefore, students must come up with a rule or a summary of key mathematical ideas they learned from the discussion. The group needs a shared understanding of what these ideas mean.

Case Study 2: Writing a Number Sentence to Represent a Fair Sharing Problem

SCENARIO: In Chapter 4, the students solved two problems: (1) If 6 children share 8 pies equally, how much pie will each child get? (2) If 8 children share 6 pies equally, how much pie will each child get? (See Chapter 4 for examples of five students' solutions.) The teacher observed that many students were confused about how to write the number sentence and mixed up the divisor and the dividend. In addition, they did not think

Continues on next page

Case Study, continue

about how the division resulted in a fractional answer as an algebraic relation between the divisor and dividend.

DISCUSSION: The teacher writes the essential information about these two problems on two chart papers and displays them next to each other to confront students about the meaning of the divisor and the dividend, its division relationship, and the size of the resulting answer.

The teacher starts the conversation by asking, "Which quotient will be less than one?" Students must think about the dividend and divisor as a number sentence. This requires students to engage in algebraic thinking.

Natalie: That one! (She points to the chart paper with "8 children share 6 pies equally," shown in Figure 5.4.)

Teacher: "You think it is going to be this one? Why, Natalie?"

Natalie: There are going to be 6 pies and 8 children. There will not be enough for them to get one whole."

The teacher writes, "The answer (or quotient) will be less than 1."

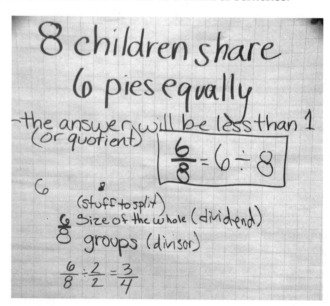

FIGURE 5.4

Problem: 8 children share 6 pies equally

ANALYSIS: The teacher scaffolds the student's explanation by writing the key information on the chart paper to clarify what Natalie means, and also makes her thinking explicit so that other students can think about her explanation. This written record of her thinking can be referred to in the subsequent discussions. By writing the word *quotient*, the teacher is introducing math vocabulary.

Next, the teacher asks the class to raise their hand if they agree with Natalie's answer. As a result, the teacher is able to quickly assess student thinking.

Teacher: Look at this problem (indicating the other chart paper, shown here in Figure 5.5)—6 children share 8 pies equally. Is the answer going to be more or less than one?

Salina: Greater than one, because each child will receive more than one pie.

Teacher: Okay. The answer or quotient will be more than one. Which number represents the things we are going to split up? Which number is called the dividend?

Student: 8.

Teacher: Okay, I'll write 8 on the chart. Let's look again at the other problem. There are 6 pies divided by 8 children equally. Can someone come up and write what they think is the "stuff to split"? We are going to call that the "size of the whole." Which of the two numbers is it—the 8 or 6? Which is going to represent the numbers that we are going to share?

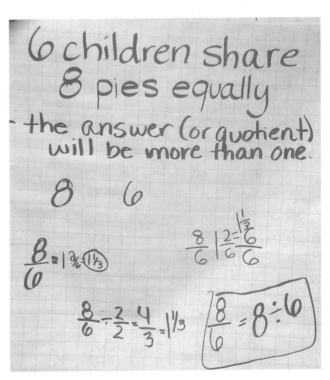

FIGURE 5.5
Problem: 6 children share 8 pies equally

ANALYSIS: The teacher is asking students to think about the problem context and identify the dividend. She refers to the dividend as the "size of the whole," or "stuff to split," wording which the students had already used to describe the dividend. A student approaches the chart and writes the number 6 to represent the dividend.

Continues on next page

Case Study, continued

Then the teacher asks students to identify the divisor in the problem situation. She asks, "What number represents the groups that we are going to split this stuff into?" Another student writes the number 8. The teacher wants students to think about the meaning of numbers in relation to the divisor and dividend. The teacher asks students to represent the division relationship as a fraction. Another student approaches the chart and writes $\frac{6}{8}$.

> *Teacher*: Thank you. What does that represent? What does $\frac{6}{8}$ represent there?
>
> *Student*: I think the six eighths represents . . . the 6 represents how many pies are there and the 8 represents how many children are there.

ANALYSIS: The student is thinking about the division relationship between the divisor and dividend. The teacher asks students to think about what the $\frac{6}{8}$ represents in relation to the problem context.

> *Teacher*: Does anyone remember what I called it?
>
> *Salina*: The size of the whole?
>
> *Teacher*: What does the 8 represent?
>
> *Student*: It could be the groups of the whole.
>
> *Teacher*: Yes, that is when we divide the whole into the groups; we are going to split up. This (pointing to the 6) represents the whole we are going to split up. We call this the dividend and this the divisor (writes next to the fraction).
>
> *Teacher*: So, I want to go back to the $\frac{6}{8}$ again. How can we say this? So, what does the line represent? (points to the fraction bar)
>
> *Student*: Division.
>
> *Teacher*: How will we say this, if we say it as a division problem?
>
> *Student*: 6 divided by 8.

ANALYSIS: The teacher wants students see the connection between the fraction representation of the problem and division by focusing on the meaning of the fraction. She inserts the math vocabulary *divisor* and *dividend* into the discussion.

Next, the teacher writes $\frac{6}{8} = 6 \div 8$. Then she writes $\frac{6}{8} = 8 \div 6$. A student makes the connection that the fractions represent division.

> *Teacher*: When you look at these two problems, what do you notice comes first in the division problem? Is it the size of whole? Or is it the groups?

ANALYSIS: This question forces students to compare both problem situations. The teacher explains that in a number sentence, the "stuff to split" appears first and the number of groups appears after the division sign. In a fraction, the size of the whole goes above the fraction bar and appears as the numerator. The number below the fraction line is called the denominator and represents the number of groups.

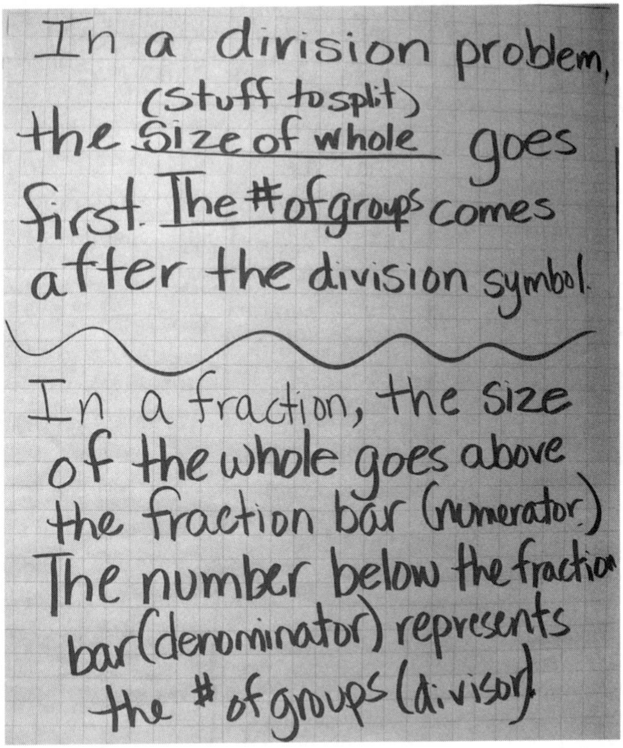

CONCLUSION: The lesson ends with the teacher and students creating a generalization, shown in Figure 5.6. In this whole class discussion, the teacher used questions to get students to think about the meaning of the divisor and dividend in relation to writing a number sentence. She scripted (wrote student responses on chart) while the students explained their answers. The class generated a rule during the whole class discussion that can be tested and applied for other problems involving equal sharing situations.

FIGURE 5.6
Class-generated generalization

Note that the case study exemplifies why a discussion should not begin with a generalization. If a discussion begins with a rule, students may end up memorizing the rule without understanding what it means. When students solve a problem during a discussion, they develop an understanding of the rule, which they can apply it in other contexts. This also means that students are more likely to remember the rule.

Chapter Summary

The questions the teacher asks during a discussion depend on the purpose of the lesson and the situation based on the classes' disposition and understanding. It is important to select the right problem to start the discussion. Problems should not be too difficult or too simplistic; they must also have the potential for mathematical issues to emerge that fit with larger mathematical goals and student understanding. Once a problem has been posed to get the discussion started, the discussion should progress through the three levels of sense-making in discussion as presented in this chapter. The first level involves making thinking explicit. Selected students share their reasoning while ensuring everyone in the class understands the explanation. The second level requires critical analysis of student solutions in order to make mathematical connections between different ways of solving problems. During this phase, students can address misconceptions and errors in thinking. The third level of understanding involves developing more abstract mathematical ideas and skills that can transfer into new situations. Carefully sequencing how students present solutions and discussions makes it easier for students to make mathematical connections because they are able to follow the arguments presented.

STUDY GUIDE

Teacher questioning is critical for scaffolding the discussion to help students make mathematical connections and engage in discussion. To get you started, here is a suggested sequence of activities designed to help you think about how to effectively use teacher questioning during the discussion. Remember, don't try to implement all these strategies at once. Focus on your larger mathematical goals and student explanations to adjust your questioning.

Examine Teacher Questioning and Sequencing

1. Examine *Strategies for Your Classroom* worksheet and think about how the three levels of understanding progressively build on each other. Reflect on what is involved in sequencing a discussion where students develop rich layers of understanding.

2. Watch the two video cases provided. Using the *Reflecting on Video Clips* Questions, analyze the videos. Your goal is to be able to visualize what questioning looks like, and to think about how it supports students' mathematical understanding.

Try It Out!

Practicing Teacher

Try some of the ideas from the *Strategies for Your Classroom* in your classroom. Use the tools provided in Chapter 4 to help you plan the lesson. Focus on practicing the strategies listed in this chapter and posing the appropriate questions for your class.

Pre-Service Teacher

In your field experience setting, try some of the ideas from the *Strategies for Your Classroom* worksheet and from the Video Cases. The tools provided in Chapter 4 can help you plan your lesson. If you are observing, reflect on how the teacher used the strategies you have seen so far. How would you approach teaching the lesson differently?

Tool Box: PDToolkit

- *Case Study I:* Clarifying an Explanation
- *Case Study II:* Writing a Number Sentence to Represent a Fair-Sharing Problem
- *Video Clips:* 5.1, 5.2, 5.3, 5.4, 5.5
- *Video Case Study:* Third Grade Lesson—Using Arrays to Find Area and Perimeter
- *Video Case Study:* Sixth Grade Problem-Solving Lesson
- *Strategies for Your Classroom:* The Three Levels of Sense-Making in Discussion
- *Strategies for Your Classroom:* Sequence of a Whole Class Discussion
- Reflecting on Video Clips
- *Reflecting on Practice:* Making Mathematical Connections

VIDEO CASE STUDY

Third Grade Lesson: Using Arrays to Find Area and Perimeter

PD TOOLKIT™

for *Whole Class Mathematics Discussions*

View the video online at PDToolkit.

Ms. Tilton teaches third grade. Many students in her class are English language learners. She has two goals in this lesson. The first is to check students' understanding of key math vocabulary. The second is to have students use their prior knowledge of arrays and multiplication to find area and perimeter.

Ms. Tilton begins by having students define key vocabulary with partners; then students share their definitions with the class as Ms. Tilton writes the definitions in their own words on chart paper. Then Ms. Tilton starts the lesson by posing the problem shown in Figure 5.7. The garden is presented as an array; squares represent the heads of lettuce on the perimeter. Ms. Tilton's questioning helps guide the students towards making their own connections and understanding the "big ideas":

Video Clip 5.1 Third Grade Lesson—Area and Perimeter Using Arrays (00:16:10)

Ms. Tilton: Do we add to find the perimeter or do we multiply? Some people are saying both, some people are saying *add* and some people are saying *multiply*. What do you think? Who thinks add? Who wants to speak up and say why you would add?

Edwin: If you add. If you times [referring to multiplication] you will get the wrong number. . . . It is going to be too high!

Teacher: It is going to be too high? Anyone else have anything else to say why you would add?

Student: How come there are two 5's and you can go 2 × 5?

Teacher: Oh, so you found a different way. So, you are saying that you can go 5 × 2 because there are two 5's. Then you can go 4 × 2, and then you have the answer. . . . Can you come up and show me what you mean?

> Spongebob is planting a garden.
> plants 4 rows of lettuce with
> heads of lettuce in each row. Wh
> is the perimeter of his garden and
> How can we solve this?

FIGURE 5.7

Problem: Finding the perimeter

ANALYSIS: Two students come up to the chart paper and write different answers. Some students think that they can multiply to find the perimeter while others think they add. By posing the question and asking students to come up to the board and make their thinking explicit by writing down the answers, the teacher makes it an issue for the class to think about. She sets up the scenario for the class to engage in the critical analysis of different approaches. Ms. Tilton asks the class to predict if the two students are going to get the same answer if one multiplies the sides of the garden and one adds the sides, as shown in Figure 5.8.

Both students explain their thinking. Leslie multiplied 5×2 and 4×2 and added 10 and 8 to get 18. Hannah added $5 + 5$ and $4 + 4$ to get 18.

Teacher: So is adding wrong?

Students: No!

Teacher: Is multiplication how Leslie did it wrong?

Students: No!

Teacher: No, they both work! How interesting!

ANALYSIS: The students conclude that they can use addition or multiplication to find a perimeter of a rectangle. Therefore, students see connections between repeated addition and multiplication. In addition to this mathematical insight, they understand the meaning of the perimeter.

Ms. Tilton provided additional support for the ELLs by making vocabulary explicit and having them describe things in their own words and make connections to more formal vocabulary.

Student 1	Student 2	
$2 \times 5 = 10$	$5 + 5 = 10$	10
$2 \times 4 = 8$	$4 + 4 = 8$	$+ 8$
$\overline{18}$		$\overline{18}$

FIGURE 5.8

Two students share the strategies they used to solve the Spongebob problem.

VIDEO CASE STUDY

Sixth Grade Problem-Solving Lesson

PD TOOLKIT™
for *Whole Class Mathematics Discussions*
View the video online at PDToolkit.

Ms. Channon Toles is a sixth-grade teacher in a Title I school. In Video Clip 5.2, Sixth Grade Teacher Interview: Planning a Lesson Involving Fractions and Problem Solving, Ms. Toles explains why she chose the problem. Video Clip 5.3, Grade 6 Problem-Solving Lesson Involving Fractions, shows Ms. Toles teaching a lesson on problem solving from the NCTM Illuminations website.

Solve The Mangoes Problem as presented below before watching the videos and reading the analysis.

Video Clip 5.2 Sixth Grade Teacher Interview: Planning a Lesson involving Fractions and Problem Solving (00:01:57)

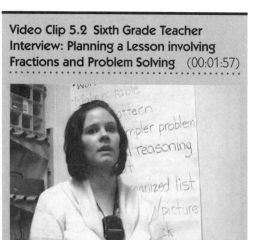

The Lesson

In Video Clip 5.2, Ms. Toles identifies that her mathematical goals are to engage students in mathematical reasoning to solve a problem involving fractions. Specifically, she wants students to use a working backward strategy where they start with the answer and work backward to figure out the initial problem. She has anticipated what students might do.

The Mangoes Problem*: Video Clip 5.3

One night the king could not sleep. So, he went to the royal kitchen, where he found a bowl full of mangoes. Being hungry, he took ⅙ of the mangoes.

Later the same night, the queen was hungry and could not sleep. She too found the mangoes and took ⅕ of what the king had left.

Still later, the first prince awoke, went to the kitchen, and ate ¼ of the remaining mangoes.

Even later, his brother, the second prince, ate ⅓ of what was then left.

Finally, the prince ate ½ of what was left leaving only 3 mangoes for the servants.

How many mangoes were originally in the bowl?

Video Clip 5.3 Grade 6 Problem-Solving Lesson Involving Fractions (00:01:57)

*The Mangoes Problem from Illuminations Resources of Teaching Math, National Council of Teachers of Mathematics. Reprinted by permission.

Ms. Toles poses the problem on the interactive white board. Then she asks students to individually think about the problem and estimate the answer. Students report their estimates and provide a justification. Ms. Toles records their answers on chart paper.

Teacher: Can you give me an estimate for the answer?

Student: 12 mangoes.

Teacher: Why do you think 12 mangoes?

Casey: Because there are 4 people, and I think each person got 3 servings.

Teacher: So you think there are 4 people, and each person got 3 servings. So where did you get the 4 servings?

Casey: From the fractions.

Teacher: So you found the common denominator?

The teacher calls on several students and writes down their estimated answers on the board. Students come up with the following numbers: 7, 8, 12, 16, 25. The teacher asks each student to explain what strategies they used and creates a record of strategies, shown in Figure 5.9.

As students work in groups to solve problem, the teacher observes that some are still struggling, so she combines the small groups into larger groups. After students have shared ideas, the whole class discussion begins. Students make their thinking explicit. One student shares a poster his group created and explains what it means.

Wyatt: We came up with a rule "*d* times 3" and *d* stands for the denominator. Each fraction is ⅙ or ⅓. We multiplied 3 times whatever the number was. We came up with 18, 15, 12 and 9 and 6 and we used that to divide into the fractions.

The teacher then poses questions to make sure that the rest of the class understands the student's explanation. In addition, students ask questions when they do not understand something.

Teacher: Any questions, comments or confusions? You need to speak up!

Casey: Why did you divide the denominator? What was it out of?

Teacher: Show us.

Wyatt: We used 6 as the highest number, because that is what it started by. So, we used $6 \times 3 = 18$. Then we divided 18 by 3 is 6. So 3 is left over.

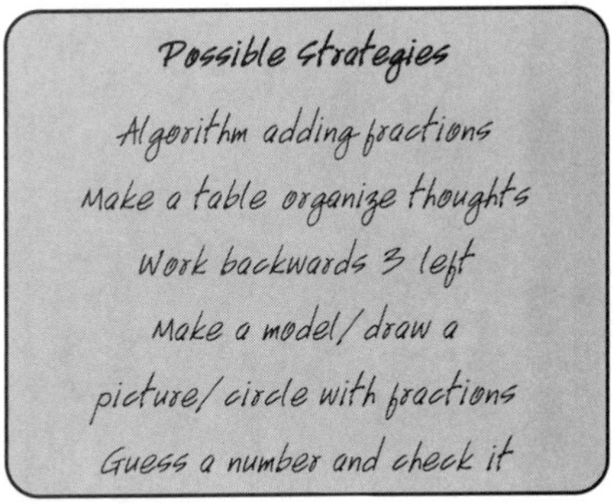

> **Possible Strategies**
>
> Algorithm adding fractions
>
> Make a table organize thoughts
>
> Work backwards 3 left
>
> Make a model/draw a picture/circle with fractions
>
> Guess a number and check it

FIGURE 5.9

Strategies for solving the mangoes problem

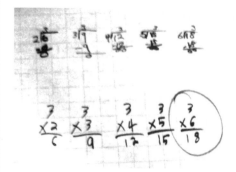

FIGURE 5.10

Solution using multiplication and division

Teacher: How did you choose 18?

Student: Because we multiplied by 3 to get 18, and 6 was the highest number.

Teacher: So, once you got 18, what did you do from there?

Student: We divided by 6.

Teacher: So, you are telling me that you did a guess and check, and you said that you had 6 that was half of 3 and you got 18? You worked backwards. You said, what is ⅙ of 18; ⅕ of 15. Is that what you did? Why did you pick these dividends there (pointing to the division problems at the top of Figure 5.10: $6 \div 2 = 3$, $9 \div 3 = 3$, $12 \div 4 = 3$, $15 \div 5 = 3$ and $18 \div 6 = 3$)? What is 6, 9, 12, 15 and 18? What do we call those?

ANALYSIS: The teacher points out mathematical insights and provides guided intervention for students to understand the mathematical idea of a "constant." The student explains that the numbers represent multiples of 3, and they chose 3 because 3 mangoes were left over in the problem.

The teacher then invites Casey to share her group's thinking. The teacher asks students not only to share thinking that worked but also to share strategies that did not work and explain why. In doing so, the teacher highlights dispositions in doing math. If a strategy does not work, then you try something else. Casey explains that at the beginning, they came up with 310 and 1860 mangoes. Understanding that these numbers were far-fetched, they began again, coming up with the drawing shown in Figure 5.11.

Casey: Then we drew a picture, and started seeing that the constant was 3. It kept going like if there are 6 gone from the bowl, there will be 3 left. If there are 9 gone from the bowl, there will be 3 left and it will be 12.

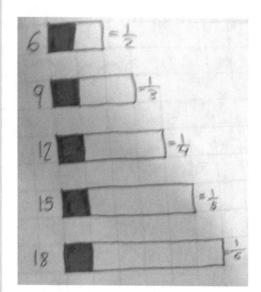

FIGURE 5.11

Solution using fraction bars

The teacher must probe students with her questioning to clarify their thinking as well as justify their reasoning. The purpose in doing so is to make sure that students understand each other's explanations. At the close of the discussion, students evaluate their strategies and estimates.

PD **pd** TOOLKIT™

for *Whole Class Mathematics Discussions*

View the video online at PDToolkit.

Conclusions

In Video Clip 5.4, Sixth Grade Teacher Interview about The Mango Problem, Ms. Toles reflects after the lesson. She mentions that she saw many students quickly pick up on the solution, but did not know how to explain their thinking. She is also surprised at how many students struggled to solve the problem. She explains how she had to scaffold their thinking and engage them in small group discussion prior to whole class discussion. She also points out that she explicitly teaches students problem-solving strategies to solve problems; these strategies are posted for students to refer to when they work with each other. The success of the lesson is evidenced in a similar problem she presents the following day, which students solve quickly.

Video Clip 5.5, Sixth Grade Student Interview on the Mango Problem, shows the student interview that took place after the lesson. Students share their perspectives of the discussion. They report that listening to others and having discussion helps them become more successful problem solvers.

Video Clip 5.4 Sixth Grade Teacher Interview about the Mango Problem (00:04:04)

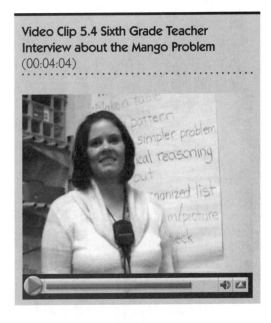

Video Clip 5.5 Sixth Grade Student Interview on the Mango Problem (00:02:32)

The Three Levels of Sense-Making in Discussion

Phase 1: Making Thinking Explicit

Questions to help students share and clarify their thinking:

- What are you thinking?
- How do you know that?
- Is there another way you can show it?
- Can you show us how you did that?
- How did you figure that out?
- Can you prove what you are thinking?
- What is the problem asking you to do?
- Is there another way to show how you solved the problem?
- Why did you think about it that way?
- Can you explain that part?

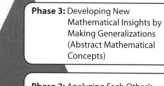

Phase 3: Developing New Mathematical Insights by Making Generalizations (Abstract Mathematical Concepts)

Phase 2: Analyzing Each Other's Solutions to Make Connections (Analyzing Low Level to More Sophisticated Reasoning)

Phase 1: Making Thinking Explicit (Explaining Reasoning)

Questions to clarify if students understand the explanation:

- Does everyone understand _____'s solution?
- Who can explain what _____ is thinking?
- Which part are you having trouble following?

Phase 2: Analyzing Solutions (from Low Level to More Sophisticated Reasoning)

Teacher questions to promote analysis and reflection:

- What do you see that is the same about these solutions?
- What do you see that is different about these solutions?
- How does this strategy relate to (the mathematical concept)?

Phase 3: Developing New Mathematical Insights

Teacher questions to promote mathematical insights:

- What do these numbers mean?
- Can you come up with a rule or summarize the key idea?
- Will the rule work all the time?
- How will you use this rule to solve another problem?

Sequence of a Whole Class Discussion

- Pose a question or problem.
- Discuss key vocabulary and clarify the general idea.
- Give time for students work in groups to solve problem and record work in a math journal.
- Transition students to a whole group.
- Call for answers, and record them on the board as students share thinking with others.
- Invite students to explain which answer they support and why.
- Call on students to ask questions or share their answer and solution on the board.
- Ask if students want to change their answer and ask for a justification.
- Arrive at consensus for the answer. Make mathematical ideas explicit.

CHAPTER 5 — REFLECTING ON VIDEO CLIPS

Video Clip 5.1: Third-Grade Lesson: Area and Perimeter Using Arrays

1. What problem did the teacher pose to start the conversation?
2. What kind of thinking and reasoning became evident? (Evaluate discussion based on three levels of meaning.)
3. How did the students participate in the discussion?
4. How did the teacher use questioning to facilitate the discussion?
5. What types of questions were used during the discussion?
6. How did the questioning lead to mathematical connections?
7. What kind of learning took place? How do you know?

Video Clip 5.2: Sixth Grade Teacher Interview: Planning a Lesson Involving Fractions and Problem Solving

1. What were Ms. Tole's mathematical goals for the lesson?
2. What are your thoughts on how she could use discussion to support these goals?
3. What kinds of problems lend themselves to discussion?
4. What is the role of problem-solving in discussion?

Video Clip 5.3: Grade 6 Problem-Solving Lesson Involving Fractions

1. What problem did the teacher pose to start the conversation?
2. What kind of thinking and reasoning became evident? (Evaluate discussion based on three levels of meaning.)
3. How did the students participate in the discussion?
4. How did the teacher use questioning to facilitate the discussion?
5. What types of questions were used during the discussion?
6. How did the questioning lead to mathematical connections?
7. What kind of learning took place? How do you know?

Video Clip 5.4: Sixth Grade Teacher Interview about the Mango Problem

1. What did Ms. Toles reflect about her lesson?
2. What surprised her and how did she adjust her discussion?
3. What kind of scaffolding did she do to help her students engage in higher level thinking and discussion?
4. What are some of your thoughts on this interview?

Video Clip 5.5: Sixth Grade Student Interview on the Mango Problem

1. What are students' perspectives' on how discussion helps them learn math?
2. Would the students have been able to solve this complex problem without talking with peers? Why or why not?
3. What are your thoughts about the student responses?

REFLECTING ON PRACTICE

Making Mathematical Connections

1. Describe the three levels of sense making in a discussion.
2. Reflect on a recent discussion you had with students. What kinds of questions did you ask?
3. What kinds of sense-making took place in that discussion?
4. What were some challenges in helping students make mathematical connections?
5. What are some strengths and weaknesses in your techniques for facilitating a discussion?
6. What are some areas you would like to improve?

Strategies for Evaluating and Improving Your Discussion

What are the next steps after having a whole class discussion? Having a good discussion alone will not guarantee that students will do well in math. We know that learning takes place when students make connections. Sequencing discussions that build on each other is critical for supporting student learning. Students need to see connections within a discussion as well as discussions over time.

Life-long learning along the *innovation* dimension typically involves moving beyond existing routines and often requires people to rethink key ideas, practices, and even values in order to change what they are doing.

(Hamerness, Darling-Hammond, Bransford, Berliner, Cochran-Smith, McDonald, & Zeichner, 2005, p. 361)

Specifically, think about what new insights your students gained from the discussion, any misconceptions or issues that need to be further addressed, and where you would like to go next with the lesson. Consider student participation as well. Are there areas that require greater student participation?

Supporting students' mathematical learning involves building on student thinking. Whether the school district requires that an entire curriculum be covered in one year or allows teachers to plan their own content, the sequence of lessons needs to be flexible and adapted to students' needs and responses.

This chapter explains tools and techniques to improve whole class discussions. Many teachers that I have worked with have reported that facilitating an effective class discussion is not an easy process. Although it takes time, the results will be rewarding.

Improving Whole Class Discussions

Facilitating effective whole class discussions requires examining current teaching practices to determine aspects of discussions that work and those that do not. This examination is a continuous process of reflection and refinement, as shown in Figure 6.1. It begins with identifying an area of whole class discussion that can be improved and practicing some of the techniques outlined in this book. Then the classroom procedures and strategies for implementing whole class discussions must be evaluated, adjusted, and expanded accordingly.

Making Classroom Teaching Visible to Improve Discussion

Improving techniques used to facilitate effective whole class discussions involves figuring out both strengths and the areas in need of growth. This requires teachers to notice what they currently do and its impact on student understanding. A teacher's ability to notice things depends on what he or she is focusing on (Jacobs, Lamb & Phillip, 2011). Not everyone "sees" the same things and makes the same interpretations. Therefore, having a lens through which to examine a lesson is helpful. Rubrics, such as those provided at the end of this chapter, can help you pay attention to different aspects of your discussion. Recording your lesson either visually or using audio only is another way for you to examine your lesson.

Refining Whole Class Discussions to Support Mathematical Learning involves:

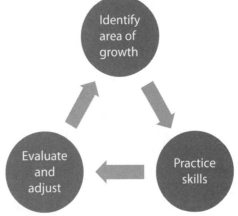

FIGURE 6.1
Refining whole class discussion to support mathematical learning

Improving whole class discussions ultimately requires us to *change* what we do that is not working. Most of us have established many classroom routines that have become automatic. We stop paying attention to what we actually do or look at the impact it has on student learning. Therefore, the first step is to make routines visible so that we can examine what is really going on.

Record the Lesson. Recorded lessons, either through video or audio recordings, are powerful tools for conducting self-evalutations. Share videos or audio segments of discussions with a colleague or math coach to develop new insights. Others might see and point out things in a video, such as certain students who need more attention or if the class needs more wait time while they work on questions.

A recording is convenient because you can fast forward to your whole class discussion and watch several minutes of the tape at a time. Many teachers have found that transcribing a brief segment of the discussion helps identify the type of conversation that is taking place. Analyzing the transcript helps identify the nature of student interaction, teacher interaction, and questioning techniques. Using a video to analyze your teaching allows examination of the classroom at a much deeper level.

Peer Observation. Ask a colleague to observe your teaching and give you feedback, or observe a colleague's class to gain another perspective on how someone else approaches a discussion. Observation rubrics are provided at the end of this chapter. Rubrics can be adapted to focus on particular areas.

Lesson Study. In a Lesson Study, a group of teachers and an expert (such as a math coach) jointly plan a lesson and set lesson goals. One teacher teaches the lesson while others observe and take notes without interfering. The lesson is revised based on the debriefing that takes place after the lesson (Fernandez 2002; Lewis, Perry, & Hurd, 2009). Next, a new revised lesson is designed and taught. This approach is particularly valuable if you are working on a series of lessons over time. The advantage of this approach is that lessons can be developed and then refined over time based on the insight of multiple perspectives. The whole group should meet regularly.

Working with a Math Coach/Teacher Leader. Working with a math coach is a good way for you to reflect and improve how you facilitate whole class discussions because math coaches have expert knowledge in teaching mathematics. They can help you critically examine your teaching techniques by asking questions and providing feedback. This can be done through observations of your discussion and working together to come up with a plan of action to help you improve how you teach.

SELF-REFLECTION QUESTIONS

1. When do you use whole class discussions?

2. What do whole class discussions look like in your classroom?

3. What are your strengths and weaknesses?

4. What are some areas that you would like to improve in your discussions?

Signs of Effective Whole Class Discussions

Facilitating effective whole class discussions can make your teaching more effective and efficient. You can address the needs of diverse learners by giving them opportunities to communicate and analyze multiple representations. Therefore, investing the time to hold whole class discussions is well worth the effort. You can introduce new information that builds on student thinking and challenges students to think more deeply about the concepts explored. The NCTM and the Common Core standards both point out the importance of communication in supporting students to learn math. A whole class discussion is only a part of the conversations that should take place within a math lesson to encourage students to build mathematical fluency and meet the standards. Whole class discussions do not replace the small group work, partner talk, or conversations with individual students. Rather, whole group discussions build, synthesize, and extend these smaller conversations. Furthermore, the whole class develops a shared understanding of mathematical issues during whole class discussions. As you continue to refine and reflect on implementing these strategies into your classroom, watch for these benefits to manifest themselves. But overall, remember that involving your students in whole class discussions will bring them closer to learning and loving math.

Chapter Summary

Once you have identified areas that you would like to improve, select one or two skills at a time to work on. Understand how these skills fit into the larger picture of supporting mathematical learning through whole class discussions. The more you practice these skills the easier it will become. The most important thing is to keep reflecting on what you are doing. Is it working? Why or why not?

STUDY GUIDE PART 1

Whole class discussions, subsequent activities, and small group discussions must build on each other to support learning. Below is a suggested sequence of activities designed to help you improve the various facets of building effective whole class discussions that support your students' understanding of mathematical concepts. Sequencing and building on student reasoning is absolutely critical to help students make connections and learn math. Even though you might have planned the perfect lesson, you may discover that things may not go as planned. Therefore, you have to adjust what you are doing and rethink your subsequent lessons.

Thinking About Next Steps

1. View the video clips from the *Video Case Study* and complete the *Reflecting on Video Clips* questions.

2. Read the case study after you have reflected on both videos. Think about how you should adjust a lesson based on student reasoning. Why it is important to pay attention to what the students are saying and doing? How will that inform your decisions on how to facilitate the discussion?

3. Try some of the ideas presented on the *Strategies for Your Classroom* worksheet. Either teach a lesson and facilitate a discussion, or observe a classroom and think analytically about the strategies outlined on *Strategies for Your Classroom*. Use the *Reflecting on Practice* worksheet to think "next steps."

Making Your Classroom Practices Visible

1. Apply some of the techniques from the chapter section *Making Classroom Teaching Visible to Improve Discussion*. These include recording yourself teaching a lesson, having a peer observe your recording or sit in on your class, forming a lesson study group, and working with a math coach.

2. Use *Strategies for Your Classroom: Refining Your Whole Class Discussion* as a guide to keep evaluating and adjusting your teaching to become more effective and efficient. This is a cyclical process that requires constant monitoring of how your class learns based on the questions you pose to scaffold their connection-making.

Tools for Improving Your Discussion

Overall, this book is designed to provide you with tools to think about the effectiveness of your whole class discussions. Once you have identified areas to work on, use the rubrics and tools provided throughout the book to improve your teaching. Re-visit each chapter as many times as you need. Use this book as a tool and adapt it to meet your teaching needs. Changing teaching methods and getting used to new routines takes time and patience. However, when you start seeing results in student learning, you will find that ultimately your teaching will become more efficient and easier and you will be able to meet the needs of students in various ability levels. Don't forget to celebrate small successes and build on what works! Best wishes in your journey towards effective whole class discussions that support student math learning.

Tool Box: PD Toolkit

- Video Clips 6.1 & 6.2
- *Video Case Study:* Second Grade Lesson on Two-Digit Addition with Regrouping
- *Strategies for Your Classroom:* Refining Your Whole Class Discussion: Long-Term Strategies
- *Reflecting on Video Clips*
- *Reflecting on Practice:* Next Steps after Holding a Whole Class Discussion
- *Reflecting on Practice:* Improving Your Discussion
- Whole Class Discussion Checklist: Informal Assessment of Student Understanding
- Student Rubric for Self-Evaluation of Whole Class Discussion
- Whole Class Discussion Participation Checklist
- Classroom Observation Checklist
- Math Discussion Rubric
- Self-Reflection Rubric for Evaluating Whole Class Discussions
- PowerPoint: Chapter 6—Strategies for Evaluating and Improving Your Discussion

PD **pd** TOOLKIT™

VIDEO CASE STUDY

Second Grade Lesson on Two-Digit Addition with Regrouping

Video Clip 6.1 Second Grade Lesson: Two-Digit Addition (00:16:36)

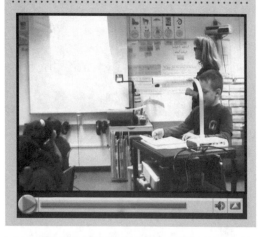

Video Clip 6.2 Teacher Interview: Ms. Akbar (00:05:10)

PD **pd** TOOLKIT™

for *Whole Class Mathematics Discussions*

View the video online at PDToolkit.

Before you read the analysis, watch Video Clip 6.1, Second Grade Lesson on Two-Digit Addition with regrouping, and Video Clip 6.2, Teacher Interview: Ms. Akbar, and reflect on the questions provided on the *Reflecting on Video Clips* worksheet. Once you have thought critically about these videos, read the rest of the case study.

The Lesson

Ms. Akbar works at a Title 1 Elementary School in Reno, Nevada. About one-third of her students have Individualized Education Plans (IEPs) and about one-fourth have limited English proficiency.

Ms. Akbar's goal is to introduce her second-grade students to the partial sums method. Her plan is to have students discover this method of addition on their own. Students are given base-10 blocks to use as they individually work to solve an addition problem involving two digits.

Ms. Akbar begins the lesson by asking students to solve the problem 27 + 48. She chooses this particular problem because it involves re-grouping, a concept she hasn't formally introduced to her students yet. In previous lessons, the students have done two-digit addition without re-grouping. Students work at their desks to solve the problem, and then share their solutions during the whole group discussion. The first student, Jacob, uses his Hundred Chart to figure out the answer. He adds the 20 + 40 to get 60. Then he adds 8 to make 68. He counts 7 more up from 68 to get 75.

After the teacher asks for other solutions, Tristen presents his solution. He concludes that the answer is 409. His solution is illustrated in Figure 6.2.

Tristen explains that he built the number 20 by using two rods representing 10 units. Next, he adds 9 to get the 29 and counts 27 individual blocks. (He had incorrectly written 29 instead of 27). At this point, he pauses, because he is unsure about how to proceed.

Tristen shared his explanation. He had recorded the following strategy in his math notebook:

2	0
2	9
4	9

409

FIGURE 6.2
Tristen's explanation

ANALYSIS: It appears that Tristen added 20 and 20 to get 49 and then concluded that he needed to add the zero in there, arriving at 409. When asked why he got 409, he explains that he was using "partial sums method." This is an example of a student applying a rule without understanding the meaning behind it. Tristen has some knowledge of addition but his answer does not make sense.

At this point, Ms. Akbar has to decide how to proceed. She has to consider what Tristen did understand and what he did not. She must also think about how other students can benefit from the how the rest of the discussion proceeds. She instructs Tristen to work through the problem again and poses questions to the class in an effort to keep them involved and help them define their own thought processes.

Ms. Akbar then asks another student to help Tristen figure out the answer in an easier way. She points out that Tristen has counted out 27 individual blocks, thus validating what he did correctly. She also makes explicit how the 27 unit blocks relate to the problem context.

Teacher: How can we help Tristen add 48 in there? He's got 27 already. How can he add 48 to that?

Student 3: With the 10's and the 1's.

Teacher: Ooh, the 10's and 1's. How can you add them?

Student 3: You can do 4 tens . . . and then 8 cubes and add 27 to it.

ANALYSIS: As the student explains, Ms. Akbar models the explanation with blocks so that the rest of the class can visualize the explanation. She asks Tristen to further explain how to physically add the 27 individual blocks, the 4 rods, and the 8 blocks. After he works with the blocks, she asks Tristen to return to his desk to figure out the answer.

After demonstrating the simpler method, the teacher moves to a more abstract method by asking Thea to explain her method. Thea correctly solves the problem using informal methods to represent the 10's and the units. She explains that she added 2 + 4 to get 6 and then added 7 + 8 to get 15.

Teacher: How does 7 + 8 equal 75?

Student: I had 60 and I added 15.

Teacher: What do you mean 60? You have a 2 and 4 (pointing to Thea's writing).

Thea explains that the 2 + 4 make up 60 and that after she got that, she counted up and re-grouped the 7 + 8 as 7 + 3 + 5. Thea's conclusion is that the answer is 75.

Ms. Akbar asks students to put their thumbs up if they agree with the answer. Some students put their thumbs up while others do not. Ms. Akbar asks if anyone else added the 10's first. Six students raise their hands. Cameron comes up and provides the same explanation as Thea.

ANALYSIS: Ms. Akbar discovers that students have some background knowledge and strategies to add two–digit numbers with re-grouping. As she explains in Video Clip 6.2, one of her goals was to get students to develop more efficient ways to solve the problems than individually counting all the blocks. She wants to help her students understand the concept of trading 10 individual blocks for one rod representing a unit of 10.

She asks the class to build a model using base-10 rods to explain what the numbers in the problem represent. In doing so, she is asking students to connect their written number symbols with the place value models. Students look at 6 rods, which represent 60, and 15 blocks.

Teacher: How that can equal 75?

Student: The 15 has a 10 in it. Then you just add the 10 and it gets 70, and you have 5 ones left over.

The student further explains that you can trade 10 individual blocks for one rod and add it to the 60 and get 70. Then you add the 5 to the 70 and get 75.

Teacher: Who can show me that? Alandro, come on up and show me that.

Alandro: You take 10 of the blocks, and trade them for a long one and then you have to use the rest of the 5's, and that will be 75.

Ms. Akbar clarifies what the student said and demonstrates how 10 individual blocks can be traded for one long base-10 rod. Then she asks the students to explain what she just modeled. One student replies, "We traded."

ANALYSIS: Ms. Akbar provids her class with guided intervention to scaffold student understanding. Students now have the opportunity to see that trading 10 individual blocks for 1 base-10 rod is a more efficient way to keep track and count. In addition, students have the opportunity to make connections to standard notation for adding two-digit numbers. Students are also able to make connections between the written symbols and the model to understand re-grouping.

Conclusion

In Video Clip 6.2, Ms. Akbar reflects on the lesson and explains the prior knowledge that students had, their reasoning strategies, her mathematical goals, and what she would do differently next time. When asked about the role of manipulatives in student explanations, Ms. Akbar observes that the manipulatives help students explain their thinking. She points out that it was hard for other students to understand the explanations by simply looking at the numbers alone.

> *Ms. Akbar:* Some of them already knew what to do without realizing what they were doing. It is interesting, because last week they could not do that. They had 5 or 6 digits in there that they were adding up instead of carrying. I am not sure when they transferred over. It was really hard to get them to state why they did what they did, without the extra one in the 10's place. I have half the class that understands it, but do not know why they understand it. Then I have the other half that does not understand it. . . . I thought for sure that they would really understand about adding with base-10 blocks. I did not know that [they did not understand] until we started discussing.

ANALYSIS: Ms. Akbar used formative assessment to make decisions on how to facilitate the discussion. She used several strategies such as listening to student explanations and having students demonstrate their understanding by explaining with models and writing. In addition, she did quick surveys of class understanding by having students show if they agreed with something or disagreed by giving a thumbs up or thumbs down. Using these methods, she was able to identify that "half the students got it," but did not quite understand "why" and the other half were confused. In addition, she also reflected on what she would do during her next discussion, concluding that she needs to spend more time with the students going over the place value and trading concepts. She explained that she can only plan a lesson two days in advance, because the discussions drive what must be covered in the next day's lesson. Reflecting is valuable for thinking about what the students understand, don't understand, and for mapping out your next steps.

CHAPTER 6 ••••••• **STRATEGIES FOR YOUR CLASSROOM** •••••••

Refining Your Whole Class Discussion: Long-Term Strategies
Monitoring and Adjusting your Teaching to Increase Efficiency and Effectiveness Takes Time to Develop.

Remember:

- Start with small pieces of strategies.
- Identify areas of growth.
- Select strategies to implement in the classroom.
- Monitor and adjust techniques through evaluation.
- Seek the support of colleagues, math coaches, and others.
- Celebrate small successes and build on them.

**Refining Whole Class Discussions to
Support Mathematical Learning involves:**

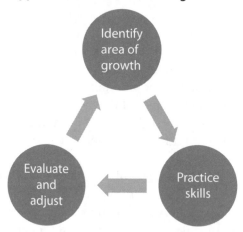

Refining Your Whole Class Discussion: Making Teaching Visible

- Record yourself teaching a lesson and analyze what is working and what needs improvement.
- Ask colleagues to observe a lesson and offer feedback.
- Observe another teacher's classroom to gain insights into other methods.
- Work with a math coach or lead teacher.
- Focus on one specific area at a time.
- Take small steps and work on them until you get results.

REFLECTING ON VIDEO CLIPS

Video 6.1: Second Grade Lesson on Two-Digit Addition with Regrouping

As you watch students explain their reasoning, consider the following questions:

1. What does the student understand mathematically?
2. What is the student confused about?
3. What would be a potential teaching point?
4. What questions might you pose to get students to clarify their misconceptions or confusions?
5. What learning took place?
6. How did the teacher use questioning to facilitate connections?
7. How did the teacher address misconceptions and errors?
8. How would the students have responded if the teacher started the discussion by showing students the "step by step" procedure for using the manipulatives to model the problem?
9. How does allowing students to struggle support learning?
10. If you were the teacher, how would you have responded?
11. What are her next steps?

Video 6.2: Teacher Interview: Ms. Akbar

1. How did Ms. Akbar use her informal assessment of student reasoning to change her questioning?
2. How did the teacher support students to make connections between the problem, manipulatives, and the written symbols?
3. What insights did you gain from listening to the teacher interview?
4. What would you do if the discussion took a different direction than expected? How would you prepare for such situation?
5. What would you do next if you were the teacher?

REFLECTING ON PRACTICE

Next Steps after Holding a Whole Class Discussion

1. What errors and misconceptions did students have during the discussion? How can you check their understanding in the next lessons?

_____

_____

_____

2. What mathematical insights did students gain during the lesson? Consider how you can build on these new insights.

_____

_____

_____

3. What areas of student participation can be improved? How can you assess whether students understand the reasoning of their peers?

_____

_____

_____

4. What are the goals of the next lesson? Do they build on the goals and skills in this lesson?

_____

_____

_____

5. What additional considerations and concerns do you have?

_____

_____

_____

Improving Your Discussion

1. Use some of the strategies listed in *Making Classroom Teaching Visible to Improve instruction* to examine your teaching. Identify areas of your teaching you would like to improve.

2. Make a list of strategies you would like to work on. You can refer back to the chapters that discuss these strategies in detail. Remember to make small goals and implement them. Don't try to do everything at once.

3. Create a plan. How are going to make these improvements?

   a. What strategies you are going to work on?

   _____

   _____

   _____

   b. How are you going to monitor your progress?

   _____

   _____

   _____

   c. Identify what supports and resources you need to make this happen.

   _____

   _____

   _____

   d. How are you going to celebrate your successes? (Remember that these strategies require practice over time. So be patient and celebrate the small achievements!)

   _____

   _____

   _____

PD **pd** TOOLKIT™

Whole Class Discussion Checklist: Informal Assessment of Student Understanding

This checklist is designed so the teacher can record students' level of understanding and proficiency in a math concept. Make sure you are very clear about the concept that you are assessing. Mastery means that the student has understood the concept. If the majority of students have mastered a concept, then spending time discussing something they already know is not an efficient use of class time. This checklist can let you know the trends of understanding and proficiency in your math class.

Mathematical Goal: _____ **Date:** _____

Student Name	Mastery	Developing	Not Yet	Notes

Student Rubric for Self-Evaluation of Whole Class Discussion

This rubric is designed for students to self-assess how they participate in whole class discussions. It also explicitly lets them know how you would like them to participate in a discussion. This rubric can be used by students to set personal goals and monitor how well they are progressing towards their goals. This can be used periodically in the classroom whereas the rubric in Chapter 3 can be used for daily monitoring until students get used to the classroom routine.

Name: _____ **Date:** _____

	4	3	2	1
I clearly explain my thinking to others.				
I listen and think about other student explanations.				
I analyze and think critically about other explanations presented.				
I reflect on my own strategy when listening to others.				

4 = All the time
3 = Sometimes
2 = Sort of
1 = Never

Comments about what I learned:

Whole Class Discussion Participation Checklist

This checklist is intended to help the teacher identify which students participate in discussion. Once students who do not participate in discussion are identified, reflect on why these students are not participating and try some of the strategies provided in the book to encourage their participation. The notes column allows you to record your findings.

Student Name	Participates in Discussion	Participates Sometimes	Does Not Participate	Notes

Classroom Observation Rubric

This rubric can be used by you or others (such as a math coach) to provide feedback on the whole class discussion. This rubric provides feedback on how content is presented, the role of the teacher, students, assessment, and classroom management. There is space for the observer to write comments.

Name: _____ Observed by: _____ Date: _____

Lesson: _____

Check areas observed or focus of observation:	Comments
Classroom Interactions	
Nature of student participation	
Teacher Questioning	
Student Engagement	
Student Understanding/Sense-Making	
Focus on "big ideas," errors misconceptions or strategies to solve problems	
Logical progression of conversation to develop more sophisticated mathematical ideas	
Students critique, reflect and ask questions about ideas presented.	
Teacher Interactions	
Poses questions to facilitate thinking or clarification	
Checks for student understanding	
Adjusts conversation based on student responses	
Introduces new information based on student current understanding	
Physical Classroom Environment	
Organization of space for discussion	
Access to materials for discussion	
Space to display multiple solutions	

Math Discussion Rubric

This rubric provides feedback on a continuum towards teaching for conceptual understanding and optimizing opportunities to learning. Use this rubric to monitor whether or not the lessons are focused on teaching for conceptual understanding and helping make mathematical connections.

Name: _____ **Observed by:** _____ **Date:** _____

	3	2	1	0	Comments
Content	Focuses on big mathematical ideas and coherence between topics	Identifies big ideas but focuses on the math lesson as a set of activities to complete	Focuses on discrete isolated math procedures	No math content	
Teacher Presentation	Asks good questions: • clarifies misconceptions; • asks students to explain thought processes	Asks good questions: • has students explain their thinking processes; • does not facilitate helping students make new connections or become more efficient in their thinking	Delivers instruction procedurally Tells students what to do and think	No teacher presentation	
Students	Engaged Respond to questions: • explain reasoning; • make connections between other students thinking; • demonstrate number sense and are able to think flexibly	Able to follow rules and apply with understanding	Follow rules to do math problems without understanding; unable to think flexibly about the math; do not have a number sense	Not doing math	

See key on next page

Math Discussion Rubric *continued*

	3	2	1	0	Comments
Students (continued)	• ask questions • show evidence of metacognition, reflection, self-correction				
Informal Assessment and Adapting	Teacher responds to students questions, problem solving and adapts teaching • uses variety of methods to adapt to student ability and thinking (visual, written, manipulatives)	Teacher is aware of student thinking but does not adapt the lesson to meet the needs of students.	Teacher teaches lesson by reading a script; checks to see if the students got the answer correct. Does not attend to how students are reasoning	No assessment	
Management Skills/ Teaching Etiquette	Students are engaged and on task.	Students are engaged and on task for some of the lesson.	Students follow direction but are not intellectually engaged and treat math as a set of skills.	Students are bored, not paying attention.	

3 = Teaching for conceptual understanding (students make deep connections)
2 = Attempting to teach for conceptual understanding but the lesson does not facilitate rich mathematical connections.
1 = Teaching by telling with little focus on student learning.
0 = Very little focus on math

Self-Reflection Rubric for Evaluating Whole Class Discussions

This rubric is designed to help teachers self-evaluate after whole class discussions. Use this to note any changes you made and how you felt they helped (or did not help) facilitate whole class discussion and improve your students' understanding of mathematical concepts.

Areas of Strength	Evidence/Observations	Notes
Areas of Growth	**Evidence/Observations**	**Notes**
Goals for Improving Discussion	**Strategies to Try**	**Notes**

Comments: _____

_____

_____

References

Baroody, A., Feil, Y., & Johnson, A. (2007). An alternative reconceptualization of procedural and conceptual knowledge. *Journal for Research in Mathematics Education, 38*(2), 115–131.

Boaler, J. (1997). *Experiencing school mathematics: Teaching styles, sex and setting.* Buckingham, England: Open University Press.

Boaler, J., & Brodie, K. (2004). The importance, nature, and impact of teacher question. In D. E. McDougall, & J. A. Ross (Eds.), *The Twenty-sixth Annual Meeting of The North American Chapter of the International Group for Psychology of Mathematics Education, 2,* 773–782. Toronto, Ontario.

Boaler, J., & Greeno, J. (2000). Identity, agency and knowing in mathematical worlds. In J. Boaler (Ed.), *Multiple perspectives on mathematics teaching and learning.* Westport, CT: Ablex.

Bochicchio, D., Cole, B., Ostien, D., Rodriguez, V., Staples, M., Susiz, P., & Truxaw, M. (2009). Language. *Mathematics Teacher, 102*(8), 607–613.

Bray, W. (2011). A collective case study of the influences of teachers' beliefs and knowledge on error handling practices during class discussion of mathematics. *Journal for Research in Mathematics Education. 42*(1), 2–38.

Bresser, R., Melanese, K., & Sphar. C. (2009). Equity for Language Learners. *Teaching Children Mathematics, 16,* 170–177.

Brown, S., & Walter, M. (2005). *The art of problem posing.* Mahwah, NJ: Lawrence Erlbaum Associates.

Bybee, R. (1997). *Achieving scientific literacy: From purposes to practices.* Portsmouth, NH: Heinemann.

Chapin, S., O'Connor, C., & Anderson, N. (2009). *Classroom discussions: Using math talk to help students learn.* Sausalito, CA: Math Solutions.

Cobb, P., Stephan, M., McClain, K., & Gravemeijer, K. (2001). Participating in classroom mathematical practices. *Journal of Learning Sciences, 10,* 113–164.

Cobb, P., Wood. T., Yackel, E. (1993). Discourse, mathematical thinking and classroom practice. In E. Forman, N. Minick, & A. Stone (Eds.), *Contexts for learning: Social cultural dynamics in children's development.* New York: Oxford University Press.

Cobb, P., Yackel, E., & McClain, K. (Eds.) (2000). *Communicating and symbolizing in mathematics: Perspectives on discourse, tools, and instructional design.* Mahwah, NJ: Lawrence Erlbaum Associates.

Council of Chief State School Officers & National Governors' Association. (June, 2010). Common Core State Standards for Mathematics. Retrieved online. http://www.corestandards.org/the-standards/mathematics

Fernandez, C. (2002). Learning from Japanese approaches to professional development: The case of lesson study. *Journal of Teacher Education, 53,* 393–405.

Fosnot, C. T. (2005). Constructivism revisited: Implications and reflections, In C. T. Fosnot (Ed.), *Constructivism: theory, perspectives,*

References

and practice (2nd ed.). New York: Teachers College Press.

Franke, M., Webb, N., & Chan, A. (2009). Teacher questioning to elicit students' mathematical thinking in elementary school classrooms. *Journal of Teacher Education, 60*, 380–392.

Gravemeijer, K., & van Galen, F. (2003). Facts and algorithms as products of students' own mathematical activity. In J. Kilpatrick, W. G. Martin, & D. Schifter (Eds.), *A research companion to principles and standards for school mathematics* (pp. 114–122). Reston, VA: National Council of Teachers of Mathematics.

Hammerness, K., Darling-Hammond, L., Bransford, J., Berliner, D., Cochran-Smith, M., McDonald, M., & Zeichner, K. (2005). How teachers learn and develop. In L. Darling-Hammond & J. Bransford (eds.), *Preparing teachers for a changing world: what teachers should learn and be able to do.* (pp. 358–389). San Francisco: Jossey-Bass.

Hardin, C. (2011). *Effective classroom management: Models and strategies for today's classrooms.* Boston: Pearson.

Hiebert, J. (2003). Signposts for teaching mathematics through problem solving. In F. K. Lester, Jr. (Ed.), *Teaching mathematics through problem solving: Prekindergarten – Grade 6* (pp. 53–61). Reston, VA: National Council of Teachers of Mathematics.

Heibert, J., Carpenter, T., Fennema, E., Fuson, K., Wearne, D., Murray, H. (1997). *Making sense: Teaching and learning with understanding.* Portsmouth, NH: Heinemann.

Jacobs, V., Lamb, L., & Philipp, R. (2010). Professional noticing of children's mathematical thinking. *Journal for Research in Mathematics Education, 41*(2), 169–202.

Jenson, A. (2008). An investigation of relationships between seventh-grade students' belief and their participation during mathematics discussions in two classrooms. *Mathematical Thinking and Learning, 10*, 68–100.

Kazemi, E., & Stipek, D. (2001). Promoting conceptual thinking in four upper-elementary mathematics classrooms. *Elementary School Journal, 102*, 59–80.

Lamberg, T. D., & Middleton, J. A. (2009). Design research perspectives on transitioning from individual microgenetic interviews to a whole class teaching experiment. *Education Researcher, 38*(4), 233–245.

Lambert, M. (2001). *Teaching Problems and Problems of Teaching.* New Haven, Conn: Yale University Press.

Larrivee, B. (2008). *Authentic classroom management: Creating a learning community and building reflective practice.* Boston: Pearson.

Leinhardt, G, Steele (2005). Seeing the complexity of standing to the side: Instructional dialogs. *Cognition and Instruction, 23*(1), 87–83.

Lewis, C., Perry, R., & Hurd, J., (2009). Improving mathematics instruction through lesson study: A theoretical model and North American case. *Journal of Mathematics Teacher Education, 12*(4). 285–304.

Martino, A., & Maher, C. (1999). Teacher questioning to promote justification and generalization in mathematics: What research practice has taught us. *Journal of Mathematical Behavior, 1*(1), 53–76.

Nathan, M., & Knuth, E. (2003). A study of whole classroom mathematical discourse and teacher change. *Cognition and Instruction, 21*(2), 175–207.

National Council of Teachers of Mathematics. (2000). *Principles and standards for school mathematics.* Reston, VA: NCTM.

National Research Council. (2001). *Adding it up: Helping children learn mathematics.* J. Kilpatrick, J. Swafford, and B. Findell (Eds.). Mathematics Learning Study Committee, Center for Education, Division of Behavioral and Social Sciences and Education. Washington, DC: National Academy Press.

Patrick, H., Turner, J. C., Meyer, D. K., & Midgley, C. (2003). How teachers establish psychological environments during the first days of school: Associations with avoidance in mathematics. *Teachers College Record, 105*, 1521–1558.

Schoenfeld, A. H. (1998). Towards a theory of teaching-in context. *Issue in Education, 4*, 1–94.

Schoenfeld, A. H. (2002). Making mathematics work for all children: Issues of standards, testing, and equity. *Educational Researcher, 31*(1), 13–25.

Smith, M., & Stein, M. (2011). *Five practices for orchestrating productive mathematical discussions.* Thousand Oaks, CA: NCTM & Corwin Press.

Spiegel, D. (2005). *Classroom discussion: Strategies for engaging all students, building higher-level thinking skills,* *and strengthening reading and writing across the curriculum.* New York: Scholastic Inc.

Star, J. R. (2005). Reconceptualizing procedural knowledge. *Journal for Research in Mathematics Education, 36*(5), 404–411.

Stein, M. K., Engle, R. A., Smith, M. S., & Hughes, E. K. (2008). Orchestrating productive mathematical discussions: Helping teachers learn to better incorporate student thinking. *Mathematical Thinking and Learning, 10*(4), 313–340.

Stigler, J. W., & Hiebert, J. (1999) The teaching gap: Best Ideas from the Worlds' Teachers for Improving Education in the Classroom. New York: The Free Press.

Whitin, P., & Whitin, D. (2002). Promoting communication in the mathematics classroom. *Teaching Children Mathematics, 9*(4), 204–211.

Wiest, L. (2008). Problem solving support for English language learners. *Teaching Children Mathematics, 14*(8), 479–484.

Yackel, E. (2003). Listening to children. *Teaching mathematics through problem solving: Prekindergarten–Grade 6,* (pp. 107–121). Reston, VA: National Council of Teachers of Mathematics.

Yackel, E., & Cobb, P. (1996). Sociomathematical norms, argumentations and autonomy in mathematics education. *Journal for Research in Mathematics Education, 27*, 458–477.

Index